Monk's Reflections

Monk's Reflections

A View from the Dome

REVEREND EDWARD A. MALLOY, C.S.C.

**Andrews McMeel
Publishing**

Kansas City

02 03 04 05 06 RDH 10 9 8 7 6 5 4 3 2 1

Library of Congress Cataloging-in-Publication Data

Malloy, Edward A.
    Monk's reflections : a view from the dome / Edward A. Malloy.
    p. cm.
    ISBN 0-7407-1876-2
    1. Education, Higher—United States. 2. Catholic universities and colleges—United States. 3. College presidents—United States. 4. Malloy, Edward A. 5. University of Notre Dame—Presidents Biography. I. Title.
LA227.4.M36 1999
378.73—dc21   99-21803
                                                                        CIP

ATTENTION: SCHOOLS AND BUSINESSES

Andrews McMeel books are available at quantity discounts with bulk purchase for educational, business, or sales promotional use. For information, please write to: Special Sales Department, Andrews McMeel Publishing, 4520 Main Street, Kansas City, Missouri 64111.

DEDICATION

With love to my sisters,
Joanne Rorapaugh and Mary Long.
They have been a constant source of
support and familial affection.

CONTENTS

ACKNOWLEDGMENTS

I would like to thank Walt Collins, who assisted me with great generosity in organizing my disparate thoughts about higher education and in assuring me that I had something worthwhile to say. I also commend Matt Lombardi, who helped to shape the final text.

INTRODUCTION

I am excited to have this opportunity to share some of my experiences and considered reflections about the state of, and issues facing, American higher education. I draw upon my firsthand involvement as student, teacher, dorm person, pastor, and administrator. In particular I hope to provide some sense of what the world looks like from my desk as president of the University of Notre Dame.

I hope that what I have to say will be of interest to other university administrators, who may face challenges similar to mine, and to students, parents, and alumni, both of Notre Dame and other institutions.

My story may be representative in many ways, but it is rooted in the unique qualities and history that have shaped me along the way. I was born and raised in Washington, D.C., in the era during and immediately after the Second World War. My father was a claim adjuster for the local transit company and my mother a secretary when she was not tending directly to the raising of me and my two younger sisters, Joanne and Mary. I attended St. Anthony's Grade School and Archbishop John Carroll High School. In addition to doing well in school, I was involved in athletics and in leadership roles both in school and in the summer recreation department sports leagues.

I had the good fortune to be a member of a highly successful high school basketball team and was recruited by many major colleges and universities. In the end I chose Notre Dame, and that opened up a new world for me. I was the first in my family to go to college. While at Notre Dame I went to Latin America on three successive summer service projects, and that not only widened my interests and horizons but helped to clarify a vocational call to become a priest. After graduating with a degree in English, I entered the seminary formation program for the Congregation of Holy Cross, Indiana Province. In the course of my formation, I completed a master's degree in English and a master's degree in theology. In 1970 I was ordained to the priesthood at Sacred Heart Church on the campus of Notre Dame. I then began doctoral work in Christian ethics at Vanderbilt University, where I received my degree in 1975.

From 1974 until today I have been on the faculty of the theology department at Notre Dame, having been promoted through the various ranks of the professoriate. I was also invited, as is the tradition with Holy Cross priests, to assume various pastoral and administrative responsibilities simultaneously with my teaching duties. I was director of the college seminary program, director of the master of divinity program, and collegiate theology director at various times. I served as assistant rector in Sorin Hall, an undergraduate male residence, for five years.

In 1982 I was invited by the board of trustees of Notre Dame to become vice president and associate provost in order to prepare for other administrative responsibilities at the time of the retirement of Father Theodore M. Hesburgh, C.S.C., which was scheduled for five years later.

In 1986 I was elected the sixteenth president of Notre Dame, and I began my official duties in the summer of 1987.

I have enjoyed immensely the opportunities that I have received for leadership and service. I consider my administrative responsibilities of a piece with the other roles that I have played and continue to play. I have been blessed with good friends and wonderful support. Whatever problems I have faced and whatever crises I have had to resolve seem in retrospect to be a small price to pay. I cannot think of any other priestly or educational participation that would be more important in its own right or more rewarding in its results.

The following chapters can be divided into three major sections. In part 1 I focus on the university president. The first chapter relates some of my experience in preparing to become a president, and what lessons I have learned that might be of use to others. The second chapter is somewhat more theoretical, as I explore the various roles and responsibilities that accrue to the presidential office, no matter in what type of higher educational institution.

In part 2 I address the main professional responsibilities— teaching and scholarship—as well as those personal habits that contribute to the lifelong pursuit of learning. Chapter 3 covers a range of issues, both practical and theoretical, that flow from the primary professorial commitment to effective teaching. Chapter 4 considers research and scholarship in the broadest sense—the obligation to keep up in one's field as well as, in some institutional contexts, the mandate to contribute creatively and according to the best available methods to the development of knowledge. Chapter 5 is a sustained reflection on reading as a practice and as a form of intellectual engagement. It may be the most personal chapter in the book.

In part 3 I examine the collegiate environment. At Notre Dame we have a strong tradition of on-campus living, particularly for undergraduate students, so in chapter 6 I draw on this concrete heritage to take up residential issues that many other institutions face to some degree or another. In chapter 7 I turn to intercollegiate athletics, the glory or the shame of many campuses, depending on the events that arouse external attention. Since I was a varsity athlete myself, I necessarily touch on many opinions that have been shaped by my own history. Finally, in chapter 8 I linger over the special set of issues that arise for colleges and universities that take seriously their religious identity and mission. This chapter addresses concerns that I, as the president of a Catholic university, take with the utmost seriousness.

Monk's Reflections

Part One

The University President

CHAPTER ONE

On Becoming
a University President

When I was growing up, I went through various phases of aspiration for what career I might assume when I reached adulthood—from my youthful hopes to be a garbage man, to a police officer, professional athlete, teacher, and priest. I never imagined that one day I might serve a modern university as its president. In talking with other presidents I find that few, if any, were driven by a clear desire to one day become the chief executive officer in a higher education institution. In describing in retrospect how they assumed their present role, most presidents will see it as a combination of solid academic preparation, opportunity for leadership formation and responsibility, and good timing. It seems to be as much serendipity (or providence) as anything else.

In this chapter I think back over my own experience and reflect about the rather strange way that American university presidents are identified, prepared, and chosen.

3

Formal Preparation

Unlike most major professions in America, there is no training path for presidents or chancellors of colleges and universities. Some assume these positions after experience in the professorial ranks followed by various levels of academic administration; others come from careers in medicine, law, business, or, in a few cases, from the ranks of government, the ministry, or the military. Some presidents were spotted early in their careers as possessing unusual administrative potential, while others emerged on the scene quite unexpectedly. Some displayed high levels of ambition along the way.

The only training ground for academic leadership I'm aware of is the Fellows Program of the American Council on Education, an effort that encourages institutions to identify middle-rank administrators who exhibit a capacity to move to higher levels of responsibility. The fellows spend a year at an institution other than their own working with a mentor, usually a dean, a vice president, a provost, or a president. They are privy to most administrative meetings at their host institution, with the expectation, of course, that they will respect confidentiality. The idea is that such comparative experience will be an additional credential for higher administrative responsibility, and in fact a fairly high percentage of participants in the program have moved higher, either in their home institution or elsewhere. The fellows also benefit from joining an informal network of academics who share information about job openings and other matters of mutual interest.

Public and private institutions vary widely in the ways

they go about searching for presidents. Most states have "sunshine laws" affecting public institutions that require disclosure of the presidential finalists. The advantage of this process is that it allows for the strengths and weaknesses of the final candidates to be vetted by representatives of the different sides of college or university life; the disadvantage is that it can easily politicize the process, and many potential candidates choose not to have their names considered because of the impact the publicity could have in their home institutions. In a few cases, candidates for the presidency of an institution have lost their jobs in their home institutions because they were thought disloyal.

At private institutions, the search process is usually much more confidential. The names of those on the final slate are reserved either to the governing board or to a select committee chosen by the board. This approach minimizes political pressures and maximizes the number of persons willing to stand as candidates, though it may not bring to the surface potential tensions until after the president is in office.

I was given a training period to prepare for the possibility that I might be chosen to succeed Father Ted Hesburgh, who served for thirty-five years as president of Notre Dame. The university by-laws specify that the president be a priest of the Indiana Province of the Congregation of Holy Cross, and five years before Ted was to step down the trustees encouraged the appointment of a number of Holy Cross religious to central administrative roles in order to insure a pool of potential candidates. Thus it was that in 1982, along with two other Holy Cross religious, I was welcomed into Notre Dame's central administration as a vice president and associate provost—the number-two academic officer of the university. There I had the leeway not only to exercise the normal range of responsibilities in the provost's office but also to learn as much as possible about the broader university community. One important thing I did was conduct one-on-one interviews with all the regular Notre Dame faculty. And I participated in all levels of administrative meetings and tried to venture out as much as possible into the nonacademic sides of the university.

The search committee of the board of trustees went through a very thorough process with each of the final candidates. We had to provide a written statement of our ideas about the office, and we underwent both individual and group interviews laced with complicated questions. At the end of it all, I felt I had fairly well conveyed to the board my views of administrative leadership and my concerns and hopes for Notre Dame. In November of 1986, I was formally elected by the trustees to a five-year term, which began on July 1, 1987.

Informal Preparation

Since there's no such thing as training for college presidencies, I am led to think about factors in my personal history that helped prepare me for the role. Although my parents occupied leadership positions in a few fraternal organizations and parish groups, I did not grow up in a family that modeled the kind of leadership roles seen in corporate life, the academy, the military, or government. In grade school there weren't very many leadership roles available to me, though I did serve as a safety monitor for a couple of years and was entrusted with organizing the altar boys at my parish in the seventh and eighth grades. It was not until high school that I began to sense the enjoyment and satisfaction of leadership: I served as student body president, cocaptain of the basketball team, and coeditor of the yearbook. From these experiences I discovered that I enjoyed speaking in public, running meetings, and trying to work with fellow students toward some common goal. Representing the student body to the school principal taught me how important it is to be well prepared to argue a case.

Athletics also provided excellent preparation for leadership. If you can concentrate on a foul shot with thousands of hostile fans waving their arms at you, then you can give a talk to a comparable-sized gathering without being intimidated. There is something about the public persona of an athlete with name recognition that prepares one for similar circumstances as a leader at whatever level. You learn the skills of concentration, disciplined preparation, teamwork, and persistence.

In college, I became with each passing year more extensively involved in extracurricular activities—not just on the basketball court but also in service activities, discussion groups, and dorm politics. In my junior year I was vice president of Badin Hall and the following year was hall president. I ran for senior class president with a friend, and although we were defeated, going door to door to introduce myself to classmates and make a case for our ticket gave me a sense of what it must be like to run for public office.

One of the groups I belonged to as an undergraduate was the Blue Circle Honor Society, an interesting mix of student leaders from almost every area of campus life. We

conducted tours for visitors, ran pep rallies, were involved
in service activities, and conducted a number of social
events of our own. Membership in Blue Circle put me regularly in the company of a most engaging cross section of
campus leaders. The society had developed an interview
process for applicants, and in my junior and senior years
I was involved extensively in these interviews. I subsequently came to realize how important an administrative
skill interviewing is, and I'm thankful for my exposure to
the process as an undergraduate.

My seminary years gave me a chance to tap into other
sides of my God-given talents. After ordination I was
elected to each of our provincial chapters, which meet
every three years to conduct business on behalf of the entire province. I was also invited to be a member of the
provincial council to assist our provincial, or chief executive officer, in the ongoing affairs of the province. And I
was invited to chair a couple of Holy Cross commissions
that oversaw matters such as seminary formation and continuing education.

When I look back now, I recognize how many of the
skills acquired during my education helped prepare me for
the presidency: public speaking, the management of groups,
the clear articulation of goals and purposes, and making
hard decisions.

PRESIDENTIAL QUALITIES

When university people get together, it is not unusual
for the conversation to turn to the qualities of the ideal
president. But in real life, the perfect person seldom ap-

pears on the scene—as they sometimes say of the search process, you look for Jesus and you're lucky if you find a Paul. No chief executive officer of any complex institution has enough hours in the day or enough energy and experience to exercise all the roles the office demands with equal levels of competence and confidence. Real-life presidents always have limitations and deficiencies, and sometimes these become glaringly obvious soon after they assume office. Nevertheless, I believe certain qualities are essential for the role, no matter what the temperament or age or gender or background of the individual.

Institutional Fit

Every university possesses a unique history and set of needs, and the president must be in absolute sympathy with the hallmarks and traditions of the institution. Whether the president comes from within the ranks or from outside, he or she should be knowledgeable about the challenges and opportunities that are unique to that institution. Normally, I believe women's colleges should be headed by women presidents, historically black institutions should be headed by African-American presidents, military institutions should seek out military careerists, and religiously affiliated institutions should look to candidates who embrace the school's denominational heritage. These, at least, should be the starting point in any search process.

Institutional fit also includes intimate knowledge of those qualities that give the school a specific niche in the higher educational spectrum. If a president comes from the outside, it is important that he or she learn as much as possible about budgetary details, academic strengths and weaknesses, the quality of student life, the traditions of the institution, the hopes and dreams of alumni, and the condition of the physical plant. If what the institution needs is a hard-charging, budget-cutting reality-inducer, it would be foolish for someone with a different set of strengths to accept the job. If the institution needs a leader with strong interpersonal skills, a capacity for bridge-building and healing, and a knack for public relations, then someone not inclined to this style of leadership will make a bad match.

One aspect of institutional fit invariably is how one resembles—or doesn't resemble—the president one succeeds. Institutions look at a change in leadership as a time to tackle new sets of issues or to alter old styles of leadership—this is part of the human condition and is all to the good. Trying to replicate the outgoing president inevitably leads to disappointment. It's impossible, and not even the previous president would be the same if he or she were starting all over again. For succession to go well, the new president needs skills complementary to but different from those of his or her predecessor.

Another element of institutional fit is the nature of the newcomer's conversation with the governing board before signing the first contract. It's important that there be mutual understanding about expectations, especially for the first few years of office. When these matters are left vague, or if the president and the board should have different ideas about priorities, it can lead to strains and even crises. If the institution is highly politicized, the new president will be pressed to champion the agendas of the various camps, and someone from the outside might find this a precarious time. When the relationship between the president and the board is clear and cordial, everything else can be tended to in time; anything else is a formula for disaster.

Developed Leadership Style

A leadership style will be a function of many variables in one's personal history. If a new president has had a fair amount of experience, including other presidencies, one would expect only minor modifications in the new position. For someone relatively fresh in the top levels of administration, however, it will take time for a leadership style to emerge. The fortunate neophyte president will have mentors, perhaps a previous president or member of the board or someone who's had comparable experience at another institution. The many books and articles in print about the presidential office in American higher education are also worth space on a president's reading shelf.

It is probably safe to say that the vast majority of contemporary presidents would want to be considered collaborative in their leadership style, yet there are many versions of what collaboration and consultation mean. Higher education has a habit of endless discussions and difficulty in arriving at conclusions. Leaders in corporate life are often appalled at how long it takes to carry a proposal through all the steps of approval in the modern higher educational institution. Faculty are resistant to having decisions imposed, even after they have been agreed to by representative bodies. Students tend to favor maximum leeway in their personal behavior. The institution, moreover, is responsible to governmental regulatory commissions and approval agencies, and it must develop a budget and live within it. It must put together long-range planning documents and fundraising campaigns. Since all these tasks involve the president, the question is always how much listening is necessary prior to the decision, and to whom. When, in other words, does consultation become an excuse for sidestepping action? How an individual answers these questions defines presidential style.

Capacity to Articulate a Vision

The modern president needs to be a person who can articulate the fundamental vision that drives the institution. This might, for example, be the aspiration to be an outstanding regional liberal arts college, or the premier engineering school in the country, or a community college responsive to local needs. Whatever form the vision takes, it is imperative that the president persuasively conveys it to all appropriate constituencies—in speeches, in printed materials, in video form, and in the ongoing deliberative processes of the school.

In today's ten-year cycle of educational accreditation, most institutions will likely spend a year or two updating an institutional self-statement. This visionary document needs to be inspiring, comprehensive, realistic, and persuasive. Particularly when it comes to the fund-raising goals that often flow from such documents, the benefactor pool and/or the state governing boards must be convinced that both the goals and the fundamental vision reflect the institution's claim to distinctiveness.

Vision isn't everything, of course, but surely it is at the heart of presidential leadership.

Effective Coordination of Administration

In order to devote maximum attention to transitional priorities, most of the presidents I know prefer at the out-set to have maximum leeway in choosing those with whom they will share responsibilities. The difficulty with inherited people is that they may have a track record or a personal agenda that is not easy to reconcile with that of the new president.

Still, it's a rare president who has the freedom to change the full administrative team all at once. In most cases, this will take several years, so it's important for the incoming president to be clear in letting holdover administrators know what he or she expects. If there are obvious incapabilities or bad feelings, these need to be addressed promptly. The worst situation would be if one of the holdovers were a disappointed candidate for the office.

After I was elected but before I took office, I consulted with a number of other university presidents whose advice turned out to be quite helpful. One of the things I was told by Tim Healy, S.J., who was then president of Georgetown, was to make sure I appointed the right number of assistants. Incoming presidents, he said, often want to signal a lean and mean administrative style and thus keep their assistants to a minimum to send a message to other administrators. But he told me no one else would ever pay attention to the appropriate size and diversity of the presidential staff, and that proved accurate.

In my first year I had one assistant. Thereafter I have had a minimum of two, and now three. We have subdivided tasks in such a way that I can count on all the work being accomplished efficiently. I read all my personal correspondence and answer that portion of it that I need to do myself. The rest I pass along to one of my assistants, who fashions a response that I review before signing. Other correspondence is more appropriately answered by other administrators; sometimes they answer directly, and sometimes I ask them to compose a response for me to sign. This way I can be certain we are not giving mixed messages across the administration.

In addition to handling the endless correspondence, assistants' tasks include responding to phone calls, preparing agendas for meetings, writing reports after meetings are concluded, and serving on university committees as the president's representative. I'm fortunate to have been blessed with excellent, talented assistants who know my values, opinions, and style so well that they can act as I would if I were handling matters myself. I ask my assistants to represent me in external settings, both in the local community and at the state, national, and international levels. When I have served as chair of statewide, national, and international committees and commissions, one of my assistants has usually helped me carry out that role.

The presidential staff must be made up of highly compatible people who share similar qualities with the major administrators—patience, thoroughness, empathy, persistence. They also need to be straightforward and frank with the president when they disagree with a decision. Often they function as an early-warning system for matters that concern the president but otherwise might fall outside of his or her scope of interests or concerns.

As for the relationship between the president and the

provost, vice presidents, deans, and directors, this must be worked out over time. I meet individually with the central officers with varying degrees of regularity, and we also have group meetings of the major officers and their assistants. This, combined with regular meetings with representative campus bodies in which many of the officers also participate, makes it possible for me to have an ongoing sense that everyone is pulling in the same direction.

I have found it useful to hold summer retreats with the university's major officers and their assistants. Lasting about four days, these interludes allow us to review the previous year and plan for the one ahead. Notre Dame is fortunate to own a north-woods property on the Michigan-Wisconsin border called Land O' Lakes that makes an ideal setting for these getaways. The location offers a dramatic change from our normal work environment and provides a setting where spouses can be present and there's time for prayer, relaxation, and friendship. Our Land O' Lakes gatherings are a very important time when those who carry the heaviest burden of administrative responsibility can forge and reinforce a common identity.

In recent years I have also met during the summer with each major administrator to review the year's successes and failures. This usually begins with a written self-evaluation to which I respond, and I then bring up other matters that seem important to me. I try to be supportive and honest in these sessions. I also welcome their comments about my own performance, and I have found that these free-flowing conversations often bring forth matters that otherwise would never surface.

During my time as president, I have had one secretary/administrative assistant. Two women have filled that role successively, and both have been outstanding. I have had absolute confidence in both as regards confidentiality and the ability to function in my absence. The role of the presidential secretary is so important that choosing one deserves whatever time is necessary when the president moves into the job. Each of my assistants also has a secretary, and it is important that they, too, work together as a team. Collectively they are the most visible face of the presidential office. The way they deal with phone calls and visitors is crucial in determining how alumni, visitors, parents, and other interested parties view the presidency.

Skill in Communication

There is no talent in contemporary leadership that is more emphasized than ready and open communication. But in the contemporary university setting, the form and extent of information flow is a matter of some debate. For some members of the faculty, satisfactory communication would entail a highly detailed explanation for every major decision, while others simply want to feel they're in touch with the central campus issues and administrative priori-
,ties. Students want to be heard, especially in areas that directly affect their education and their living situation. Staff are especially concerned about work conditions and remuneration packages. Alumni and friends of the institution want to feel informed about the overall direction and fiscal integrity of the school.

One problem complicating the communication issue is the information overload that afflicts all of us. Our mailboxes are already overflowing, and E-mail threatens to usher in a new and endless stream of data, opinion, and information. It seems foolish for administrators to spend excessive amounts of time in formal communication when the important need is to be involved in consultation and active decision-making.

At a minimum, all the major groups that make up the institutional community should have periodic access to the major decisions that effect their well-being, and this should be done in a way that leaves them feeling informed. They do not need to know everything, nor need they be overwhelmed with all the steps in a decision-making process or all the points of view that were advocated in the deliberative stage of decisions.

A perennial communication problem for institutions is establishing the limits of confidentiality and the levels of information that should be confined to particular groups or individuals. It would be inappropriate, for example, especially at a private college or university, to reveal information about faculty salaries, student disciplinary decisions, or the reasons why one candidate was selected over another for a major position. Of course, confidentiality should never be used as a lame excuse, but I believe a commitment to the well-being of others and to a healthy community requires that confidentiality be respected more often than some outside agents would like.

In my effort to try to keep the university constituencies up-to-date, I employ an annual address to the faculty; reports to representative bodies of faculty, staff, administration, and students; and periodic reports on behalf of university-wide committees. I feel a greater urgency about communicating with the trustees, the representative bodies, and parents than with most external agencies.

THE RIGHT TIME TO BE PRESIDENT

I am not sure whether there is an ideal age for becoming a president or an ideal age for stepping down. My predecessor, Ted Hesburgh, became president at the age of thirty-five. I was forty-six. In retrospect, I am pleased that I was not invited to take the position until I was in my forties. This allowed me to establish myself as an academic and to engage as a pastor in the lives of students at a time when I was much closer to them in age and life experience.

I suspect it's unusual for anyone to become president of a major university earlier than his or her forties, and it's more likely to happen in the fifties or early sixties. If one enjoys good health, raw age may not be all that significant. But a president needs to be sufficiently mature to handle pressure, especially the criticism that goes along with being a public figure, and it helps to have been around the circuit a few times. During my incumbency, I have drawn frequently on my five years as a vice president and associate provost. Although I was a little removed from the center of the public eye back then, I carried responsibility for a number of committees, projects, and other administrative endeavors.

My third five-year term in office began in 1997. In 2002 I will have to decide whether to allow myself to be considered for another term. Although I would only be in my early sixties, I have seen other presidents lose fire and enthusiasm for the job, either because of difficulties they encountered or simply because they wanted to assume other responsibilities.

A priest/president presumably can continue as a liturgical leader and pastor as well as an academic. I have tried to keep my hand in as a theologian and ethicist, although there is no way, as president, that I can find time to keep up satisfactorily with the literature and the changing nature of my discipline. A long-term president might return to the departmental faculty, or might even begin another career on or off the campus.

Any president in office for multiple terms develops a certain style of administration and a network of relationships with friends and institutional benefactors. Essentially this is an asset, although there's a down side to it—since one can only concentrate on a limited number of items at once, some things inevitably get neglected or receive only secondary attention. A change in leadership helps the institution maintain equilibrium over time across a wide range of component parts and issues.

Perhaps the most important consideration in replacing a long-standing president is whether there are internal candidates around to provide a relatively smooth transition. Since the presidency at Notre Dame is restricted to Holy Cross priests of the Indiana Province, I consider it one of my responsibilities to provide opportunities for younger members of the order to gain significant administrative experience. In the end, I will have no say in who succeeds me. I hope and pray, however, that I will have the wisdom to know when is the right time to step down—both the right time for me and the right time for Notre Dame.

CHAPTER TWO

Presidential Roles and Responsibilities

The roles and responsibilities of a college or university president are diverse, demanding, and difficult to describe adequately. Most of us begin our tenure with real commitment and a desire to make a difference for the good in the life of the institution. If we are fortunate, we can concentrate our attention on the most fundamental things. We can be a persuasive advocate, a worthy representative, an effective facilitator, a persistent enabler. But even in the best of times, we make mistakes and face problems outside of our control. The test of presidential leadership is both to create a context in which the institution can flourish and to mobile the energy to face even the worst threats to campus cohesion and confidence.

DEALING WITH THE MEDIA

The president is of necessity the most publicly visible and authorized representative of the university. This role requires both preparation and professional advice. In this day of investigative reporting, it is tricky at times to know how to respond to media inquiries. Investigative reporters sometimes feel they have a right to information that others consider privileged. In times of crisis, the public relations office should normally be the prime point of contact between university administrators and the media. Some matters, even though embarrassing, have to be faced head-on; it is generally foolish to stonewall, but at the same time it is important to attempt to tell one's story effectively and fairly, and to take the initiative in telling the story to as broad an audience as possible. I accept invitations to appear on radio and television shows if I think the topic being discussed is pertinent and I have something to contribute to the discussion. Such appearances, after all, provide opportunities for Notre Dame to gain visibility as a university.

In the period when I served as vice president, I was encouraged to work with a media consultant in order to become more familiar with television as a medium of communication. I learned about the importance of body posture, facial expression, and timing. I also tried out various techniques for handling hostile interviews, probing questions, and uninformed interviewers. Radio interviews shows are less demanding than television, simply because you don't have to worry about how you look. Most of my experiences with radio have been quite positive.

The most fun I've had on television has been on the *Charlie Rose Show*. Rose is a very comfortable and relaxing host who does his homework and operates in an easygoing and engaging fashion.

Early in my presidency a crew from *60 Minutes* spent

about a week on campus filming me in a wide variety of
settings, including a two-hour, one-on-one interview with
Morley Safer. When the show finally appeared, it lasted
about twelve minutes. The part that reached the viewers
was generally favorable, but it was a lesson to me in how
much editors control the images created on television. One
of the difficulties in doing interviews as the president of
any institution is that whatever you say is accepted by the
public as the position of the institution. This can be especially tricky for a Catholic priest, because interviewers
often throw in questions about controversial church issues that have nothing to do with your role as university
president or public citizen.

Notre Dame owns a television station and a TV production company, and until recently we owned a radio station as well. Some people think we should exercise greater
control over the on-the-air content of our television station's programming. We are an NBC affiliated station, but
we also buy programming from various rerun companies.
It is primarily through the special shows we choose to air,
as well as the kind of priorities exercised in the news division, that we can have some influence on the nature of
station content. We have an obligation to provide multiple points of view on the air, but on occasion we have
discussed particular programs with the management as
they put together their annual schedules. A few shows
have seemed incompatible with our value system, and we
no longer carry them. That has not prevented them from
being picked up by one of the other stations in the area.

Our production company, Golden Dome Productions,
allows us to employ the latest and best technology to tell

the Notre Dame story to multiple and far-ranging audiences, especially in connection with fund-raising efforts and to celebrate particular events on the campus. Golden Dome also produces a respected series of half-hour shows that tackle significant issues such as racism, the world's religions, family life, the U.S. constitution, and so on. Notre Dame faculty are sometimes used in these programs, but we have also found that when the topic is interesting and important, many prestigious people are willing to appear for free. One sign of the success of Golden Dome's programming is that many of its shows have been picked up by PBS stations around the country. I'm happy to have Notre Dame identified with this effort to produce high-quality content for public consumption.

THE PRESIDENT AND THE TRUSTEES

Crucial to a smooth-running university or college is a president who works well with the institution's governing board. At Notre Dame, the board of trustees has a maximum size of sixty, not including life trustees, who are trustees emeriti. Within the board is another entity, called the fellows, composed of six Holy Cross priests and six lay people. On most matters of governance the trustees have primary authority, but only the fellows can change the university bylaws, and it takes a two-thirds vote to do it—a mechanism devised as a safeguard for the university's Catholic character and mission when Notre Dame moved to a lay board thirty years ago.

Having served with two consecutive chairs of our board of trustees, I've gained a feel for how the personality and style of the chair need to be meshed with that of the president. The two must maintain regular and thorough communication, since the chair is the prime interpreter of events to the other board members. Another important function of the board chair is to make sure that the committees are doing their jobs and keeping in touch with the appropriate officers of the university.

Because our board has national and international members, we hold only three meetings of the full group each year—two of them on campus, in the fall and spring, and the third in Florida in February. Together, the chair and I set the agenda for the full board and decide which matters are directed to the committees, which meet the afternoon before the full board convenes. I dislike major surprises either in committee or full board meetings.

As president, I am an ex officio member of our board of trustees and I also chair the fellows. Philosophically, I believe that the chief officer of the institution should always be a member of the board, but that the other officers should not. I feel this way even though in our case the provost and executive vice president are ex officio trustees, and that arrangement has worked well for us. Either way, the officers should participate in board and committee meetings. It is especially helpful when the trustees and the central administrators enjoy not only formal but also informal personal relationships; this fosters mutual confidence and eases the strains of dealing with emotionally trying situations.

One of our board's responsibilities is to review the performance of the president. In turn, it is my responsibility to review for the full board the performance of the other officers. This can get complicated, because various board members may have a vested interest in their relationship with particular officers. A better way, I believe, would be for the president to report his appraisals either to the chair alone or to the executive committee.

As for soliciting feedback about the presidential performance, it is up to the trustees to determine the format for that. I have always been comfortable providing a written self-evaluation, followed by discussion with the board, and then allowing the trustees to conduct their evaluation of me in my absence.

The worst possible situation any president can encounter is to lose the confidence of his or her board. Not only will the president's self-confidence and freedom of decision-making be diminished, but to the extent that this lack of confidence is communicated within the institution it will make presidential leadership difficult or impossible to exercise. There will always be room for disagreement in the eyes of some members of any board about particular actions or priorities of the president and central administration; this is simply a function of human differences. But there should be mechanisms in place by which disagreements are adjudicated and a consensus reached. If individual board members are still unhappy with the outcome, they should exercise restraint in voicing their disagreement publicly. Some of the worst erosions of presidential leadership I am familiar with occurred in cases where some members of a board had a disproportionate interest in matters related to athletics and tried to micromanage that narrow area of the university to the detriment of the whole.

Problems can also arise when trustees try to influence

student-admission decisions. Board members deserve the right to argue legitimately on behalf of particular candidates for admission, but they may not always appreciate how unfair it is when students enroll without the proper qualifications. These decisions are less difficult when it comes to the immediate relatives of members of board members; it is when the relationships are more indirect that the administration often feels under the gun.

PRESIDENTIAL COLLEGIALITY

Like members of any profession with a limited membership, presidents and chancellors look forward to coming together for discussion and mutual support. There are a number of national, regional, and state-level associations for college leaders, and a few that are international. I have tried to be active in many of these organizations. I have, for example, attended meetings of the International Association of Universities and the International Association of University Presidents. International meetings can be a bit trying for Americans, because they tend to be highly philosophical and theoretical. Often, scholars from certain parts of Europe seem intent at these gatherings on designing the perfect university or trying to reach consensus about the characteristics of the ideal president. Americans tend to be more pragmatic and action-oriented—it's not that we are averse to theory, but we feel bogged down if it dominates the agenda.

One fringe benefit of international meetings is the opportunity they provide for exploring distant parts of the world and becoming more familiar with the variations of higher education from one country or region to another. It is comforting for Americans to realize how difficult it is to function as a university leader in certain contexts.

For years I have been a member of the board of the International Federation of Catholic Universities, an umbrella organization for the approximately five hundred Catholic colleges and universities throughout the world. It is interesting to note that about half of these institutions are located in the United States. The circumstances of the world's Catholic institutions vary considerably from one country to another. For example, in Thailand or Taiwan or Japan, where Christians are in a very small minority, the institutions may only have somewhere between 1 and 5 percent of their student body who are Christian, and an even smaller percentage who are Catholic. These institutions see their ministry as one of service in a sometimes alien culture. Another example is India, where certain parts of the country are fairly heavily Christian but there are state-imposed limitations on the degree of independence granted Catholic universities; the state determines who the faculty are, what students can be admitted, what courses can be taught, and how exams will be scheduled. Consequently, much of the religious dimension of these institutions takes place in an extracurricular fashion.

The debates that go on among Catholic institutions in the United States, where we enjoy both a high degree of autonomy and a generally supportive alumni, are unique to this country and its traditions. In Europe, where most colleges and universities were overtly Catholic in the Middle Ages, very few now consider themselves Catholic. In some places in Europe, there are specific faculties within the overall university setting that are identifiably Catholic, such as a Catholic program in theology. Since most of the world's universities offer few opportunities for on-campus living, the ability of the university administration and faculty to influence students' values, attitudes, and behaviors is largely restricted to the curriculum itself and a few extracurricular organizations.

I have learned much from participating in the International Federation of Catholic Universities (IFCU). Perhaps its most critical role came from our conversations with the Vatican about *Ex Corde Ecclesia*, Pope John Paul II's document on Catholic higher education. Because the members of IFCU knew each other and had arrived at a consensus about what we considered desirable, we were able to have a significant influence on *Ex Corde Ecclesia* as it moved to the ultimate stages of formulation.

As for U.S. organizations, I have chaired the American Council on Education (ACE), which is the closest thing there is to an umbrella organization for higher education. In structure and governance it is a presidents' organization, although it also provides services for faculty and students and other administrators, and its annual meetings are open to the whole array of participants in higher education, including presidential assistants and those who are involved in curricular formation, fund-raising, and the challenges of intercollegiate athletics. Because ACE is so representative, I found in my years on the board and as chair that I was constantly learning about the variety that exists among the 3,500 post-secondary educational institutions in the United States. I came to know presidents of community colleges and historically black institutions and leaders of state systems of higher education. The discussions we had and the efforts we made to arrive at consensus about controversial issues always sent me home feeling better equipped to handle the challenges of my job. I also felt that when I was lobbying with the White House or Congress on behalf of higher education, I could better articulate the variety of challenges faced by different kinds of institutions because of my participation in ACE.

I have also served on the boards of or chaired the Association of Governing Boards' Presidential Committee, Campus Compact, the National Association of Independent Colleges and Universities, and the Association of Catholic Colleges and Universities. In each of these groups, schools that share a common range of interests and concerns gather for mutual support, guidance, and the articulation of policy. Each of these organizations has the benefit of a staff, normally based in Washington, D.C., who provide continuity as the leadership changes from year to year. There are sometimes deep rivalries amid the several presidential organizations, but this is not surprising since the institutions they represent are sometimes rivals for a shrinking dollar. I'm absolutely convinced that ACE and the other organizations that bring together a cross section of presidents and types of institutions are essential for the health of American higher education.

One other interesting organization I've belonged to, the Business/Higher Education Forum, has a split membership: half are presidents of academic institutions and half are CEOs of corporations and major businesses. The great advantage of the forum is that it allows people with executive-level responsibility in both education and business to come to know one another in a warm and friendly setting. This breaks down the stereotypes we all carry around. Over time, I came to appreciate the challenges faced by leaders in other institutional environments. The forum has suffered in recent years because of the difficulty in finding corporate CEOs who have the time and commitment to participate actively.

FUND-RAISING

Fund-raising is one leadership role that every university and college president must play, whether the institution is public or private. For some presidents, fund-raising becomes the hallmark of their term in office. If this talent was exactly what the institution's board of trustees was looking for, everyone will cheer, but I think it would be shortsighted to limit the role of any president simply to fund-raising. On the other hand, for a modern president to be ineffective as a fund-raiser is to invite a short term of leadership. Colleges and universities can no longer accept unenthusiastic or sluggish fund-raising performance at the top, and any president who finds it distasteful, or is unable to articulate effectively a vision of the institution that potential benefactors find attractive, should move on and pass the mantle to others.

There simply isn't enough money available either from tuition or from government sources to pay the full costs of higher education. Thus Harvard is engaged in a $2.1 billion fund-raising effort, and several schools are shooting for $1 billion. As for us, in May of 1997 Notre Dame announced the public phase of the Generations Campaign with a goal of $767 million by December of 2000. That amount is more than we raised in all our previous campaigns combined.

At one time it was almost exclusively private institutions that had regular, large-dollar fund-raising campaigns on about a ten-year cycle. Now even the flagship campuses of state university systems are engaged in fund-raising at a level comparable to the largest of the privates. In fact, the distinction between public and private has begun to break down when it comes to funding structures.

In order to raise large sums of money, it is necessary to have in place a sophisticated fund-raising operation with significant numbers of professional personnel, a lot of high-tech support equipment, and a wide and deep commitment from the school's board members and alumni. Most campaigns raise the vast majority of the dollars from a relatively small percentage of the benefactor pool. But experience has shown that those who make low-dollar gifts often become more closely tied to the university as a result, and later may make larger benefactions.

Presidential roles in fund-raising vary considerably from one institution to the next, of course. Some presidents serve as the primary representative of the institution in all solicitation efforts, on campus or off, large or small. To do this, however, they must relinquish hands-on participation in the academic, student, and fiscal administration of the institution, and that's unfortunate because fund-raising should be just one role among many played by the modern president. This trap can be avoided with excellent personnel in the school's university-relations operation.

At Notre Dame, an efficient and highly motivated group of professionals participates directly and indirectly in our fund-raising ventures. Some have the duty of telling our story effectively. Others conduct research into potential benefactors—personal, corporate, and philanthropic. Others plan the logistics for events. Still others keep us in touch with corporations or foundations that might be sources of gifts.

One of the most critical fund-raising areas for any institution is garnering annual unrestricted gifts. Notre Dame donors who pledge $1,000 a year in unrestricted gifts become members of an elite group we call the Sorin Society, named for the school's founder, and a subgroup within the Sorin Society is made up of supporters who give $3,000 annually. To encourage deferred gifts, we have established the Badin Guild, named for a pioneer priest in the Midwest.

One of the most effective fund-raising tools we have fashioned is a process we call Fly-In Weekends. These events are an opportunity for major-donor prospects to spend close personal time with the president, provost, executive vice president, vice president for university relations, and director of development. Six to nine couples are flown to the campus on these weekends, arriving late Friday for a reception and dinner and returning home Sunday. During the visit, we try to get them in touch with many aspects of the university, including student scholarship recipients who speak at one of the meals. I am intimately involved in these weekends—overseeing the conversation at the Friday dinner, hosting a reception in my office on Saturday afternoon, then celebrating and preaching at a Mass in a chapel that replicates the original campus chapel. Finally, I welcome the guests for a Saturday dinner on the top floor of our library building, where I offer some reflections.

Although the guests generally know why they are invited, most have not yet been engaged in the level of support that wc intend to request of them after the weekend is over. I very seldom ask anyone for money personally. My role is to establish rapport with the visitors and provide an attractive, engaging vision of the university and its aspirations. An early follow-up visit is made to each guest by our vice president of university relations, our director of development, or one of our major staff people.

On a few occasions invitees have declined to participate, but in the main these events have been amazingly successful. The average gift from participants runs quite high, and the process is an important reason for the success of our fund-raising.

Another way in which I try to assist the fund-raising effort is by giving a couple of days of my time per year to each of our regional development directors. They are free to schedule me as they wish on these occasions, and they generally put together a series of events in places like New York City or Los Angeles or Chicago or Dallas or Atlanta, at which I talk about Notre Dame and discuss our hopes and dreams with corporate leaders, heads of philanthropic foundations, local government leaders, and Notre Dame alumni and friends.

Usually these events are hosted by a member of our board of trustees or some other major benefactor, and they often produce better turnouts than we can match on campus. With plenty of leeway, our regional development directors have been successful in opening up possibilities and prospects we might never have thought of otherwise.

One special advantage we enjoy at Notre Dame is the opportunity to schedule the fall meetings of the board of trustees and college advisory councils prior to home football weekends. This creates a special inducement for members to attend. I have heard from many parties that Notre Dame does an outstanding job of hosting such groups on campus. We set a high standard in dedicating new buildings, installing new professorships, and celebrating new scholarships. We try to express our thanks to people who have been supportive in multiple ways, including picture taking, the awarding of plaques, and providing donors with a chance to witness what they have made possible.

When I'm asked what percentage of my time is devoted to fund-raising, I find it impossible to answer. In one sense, I could say almost all my dealings, especially with people who are not university employees or students, are connected with fund-raising. As the first representative of Notre Dame, I must establish rapport with as broad a cross section of present and potential supporters as I can. Every time I give an invited lecture to a new audience, fresh contacts may open up. When I meet with local alumni clubs, I try to reinforce the warmth of their relationship with the institution. During the public phase of a capital campaign, I'll visit from seventy to a hundred cities for special events, and here the fund-raising focus will be sharper. Ultimately, fund-raising is a shared responsibility among the officers, trustees, and other central figures of the university, but there is no getting away from the importance of the president's involvement in and oversight of all of these activities.

One question I'm sometimes asked is this: Would the university ever say no to a gift? The answer is, we would and we have. For example, we would never accept money from narcotics traffickers, persons connected with organized crime, or individuals or companies that had made their money illegally or in immoral ways. Nor do we give potential benefactors the right to dictate the terms of a gift if those terms seem to be in violation of normal standards of the academy. Since there are, at any given moment, multiple areas in need of benefaction, it's usually not hard to find a good fit between our needs and the interests of the donor.

One duty for which benefactors should hold presidents accountable is seeing that gifts are applied to the purposes for which they were given. It is simply not acceptable to manipulate funds or finagle the reporting mechanisms. Unrestricted gifts, obviously, may be applied wherever the leadership sees a need. In addition, there are occasions when money was given in the past for purposes no longer pertinent to an institution—for example, a scholarship endowment in an area of academic life that no longer exists—and in such situations, with proper review, it is appropriate to redirect the funds to some area of current need.

I am confident that Notre Dame will raise the $767 million we've targeted for the Generations Campaign because I have faith in the commitment of those friends who will make it happen and in the excellent support staff who prepared for the campaign. In some ways, it is easier to raise money once momentum has been established—

people like to contribute to institutions and causes they see developing on a positive trajectory. I believe our earlier campaign successes have given us that kind of momentum.

Like any president, I am called upon from time to time to help other not-for-profit institutions and organizations to raise money, and I have tried to respond to such calls. I have, for example, given many speeches throughout the country on behalf of Catholic primary and secondary education. I have spoken on behalf of Catholic hospitals and homeless shelters and other social services. And I have tried to raise money on behalf of a number of the national organizations I've chaired or participated in. Never have I found these activities to be in conflict with my primary responsibility to the University of Notre Dame.

We are fortunate in the United States to have a robust tradition of philanthropy, not only for the benefit of education but for a host of causes. It is part of the spirit of this nation to support the institutions we believe in. Alexis de Tocqueville in his famous work *Democracy in America* was prescient in describing us as a people who establish a group for almost every cause. We believe in getting involved to make a difference. This cultural characteristic is reinforced by America's tax laws, which allow individuals and groups to write off charitable donations. It would be very unfortunate for U.S. society if this stimulus were to be lost.

The President as Decision-Maker

Like any other public figure, the president of a college or university will sometimes be criticized for his or her performance or style of dealing with crises or complex decisions. If one is fortunate enough to be involved in an institution that enjoys relatively good circumstances, the number of these unpleasant moments will be minimal. But it is simply the nature of complex institutions that things will sometimes go wrong, and the leader has to be able to handle the criticism that follows.

The kinds of decisions that can lead to controversy are numerous. Every year when tenure and promotion decisions are made, some percentage of those who receive negative news will feel aggrieved, no matter how extensive the process that preceded it. Sometimes those who are denied promotion or tenure will try to rally support, claiming that the process was flawed or that individual participants, including the president, have prejudices based on gender or age or religious affiliation or sexual preference or anything else that might elicit sympathy and support. At Notre Dame I am the ultimate decision-maker on all faculty hiring and tenure/promotion cases, a responsibility I take with great seriousness. I am comforted, however, by the several layers of advice that I receive before the file comes to me for final decision.

In very few cases is there anything but a clear-cut judgment to be made; most decisions are either overwhelmingly positive or clearly negative. But there are always a few cases in which circumstances point to further discussion. Sometimes problems arise because one academic area of the university is perceived to have lower standards than others. Or there can be complicated social dynamics among those making recommendations at the department or college level. In the end, all the president can do is look at the evidence as fairly as possible and then, after soliciting whatever further advice might be appropriate, make a decision. That is the way I proceed in these matters.

I find it helpful to possess a background of involvement in the faculty-promotion process through so many cycles of years. When there is a split departmental vote, experience teaches you how to interpret the candidate's dossier and what to look for in outside letters. The provost and I spend significant amounts of time discussing the most troubling cases, because we know that tenure decisions can be worth millions of dollars to the institution over the course of a faculty member's lifetime of service. Yet once the decision is made, I never find myself beset by doubts or sleepless nights. As in all processes that involve human agents, I simply try to be as alert and all-encompassing as possible in the perspective I bring to my decision.

In matters of student discipline that involve dismissal penalties, I am the court of last resort. There is a process of adjudication that takes place within the Student Affairs office, of course, and my primary responsibility is to make sure all policies and procedures have been adhered to. I am not expected to make a decision about guilt or innocence, but if I'm not satisfied with the fairness of the process, I remand it back to Student Affairs.

One of the touchiest situations any president has to face in cases of student misconduct is the reaction of both the alleged victim and the alleged perpetrator and their families. In this day and age, there is often a rush to litigation, since there is always some person or family unhappy with any decision.

Disciplinary cases can also be complicated by the publicity they attract when the accused student is relatively well known, such as a student-athlete or the son or daughter of a famous person or someone who represents a certain category of individuals. I have not felt any particular emotional pressure in these cases, but one cannot help being aware that one's decision will probably be hashed over in the press, perhaps negatively.

Every president gets a fair amount of mail and unsolicited phone calls, some of it from people with complaints. If parents or visitors think they were treated rudely by campus security, or a student is angry about the way a rector dealt with a situation, or a benefactor does not think he or she is sufficiently appreciated, then it is my responsibility to address the issue.

Beyond that, a president needs to decide how available to be—in person, on the telephone, or via E-mail. My policy is that I will see any student, staff member, faculty member, or parent when a convenient time can be arranged. One of my secretary's roles is adjudicating people's claims on my attention. In some circumstances they are content to have someone else address their concerns, and so my three assistants or other members of the administration may respond to a given complaint.

Some percentage of the people who want access to a president do not deserve any particular recognition. Some have no connection to the institution and simply want someone to pay attention to them. Some are mentally ill or have schemes for a screwball invention or want to warn the world of attacks by Martian invaders or are convinced they're being manipulated by the CIA through electronic probes in the brain. One of the most common sentences used to introduce a complaint is, "How can you as a Catholic university . . . ?" The implication is that we have abandoned our principles in kicking someone out of school or not giving free tuition to a worthy student or not promoting a faculty member or not overturning a flunking grade. This approach makes rational dialogue elusive.

Some of the mail I get is also received by hundreds of other presidents simultaneously. People with enough resources are satisfied just to have someone read their latest poem or respond to their prize theory. Making decisions about who deserves time or an official response is one of the geniuses of presidential leadership. One can easily spend a disproportionate amount of time with the alienated or those who suffer from insomnia or people in state prisons.

I answer all correspondence as quickly as I can, and I respond to legitimate telephone calls on the same day if at all possible. I have made a decision not to be a big E-mail user, partly because I'm not a big computer user and partly because I found when I first went on-line that I received too much unsolicited mail. I prefer to respond to people in other ways.

I generally have an easy time living with my decisions when they are preceded by preparation and discussion. Even if such decisions are not well received, I feel confident that I did the best I could. What is aggravating is having to deal with matters I could do nothing about. My normal response is to apologize, if appropriate, and to assure the grievants that nothing was done deliberately to harm them or make them unhappy. Sometimes this is enough to satisfy the injured parties, but not always.

MATTERS OF STYLE

Certain rhythms of a president's life are set by the nature of the institution and its annual cycle. Others flow from the president's style. For example, I am a night person and not much good in the morning; therefore there are no such things as "power breakfasts" at Notre Dame, at least not with me as a participant. Before I assumed the presidency, I often stayed up until 2 or 3 A.M. Now I go to bed closer to 12:30 or 1 A.M. In order to handle the difference between my schedule and that of my secretary, I often leave dictated tapes or other materials in my office before I go to bed. I usually show up at the office some time around 9 A.M. Since many of my responsibilities take place over lunch or dinner or in the evening, this schedule works out reasonably well.

One of the most valuable bits of advice I got from other presidents was to make sure I get enough sleep, and for the most part I try to get more sleep now than I did when I was a faculty member and an assistant dorm rector. As a public person subject to a certain amount of analysis by observers, I feel it's important to look fresh and energetic and never sleepy or yawny.

My responsibilities in regards to travel often take me away from the routines of my religious community and the dorm in which I live. As someone absolutely committed to the daily Eucharist, this means I sometimes find myself celebrating Mass alone in hotel rooms. Some theologians have difficulty with this sort of liturgical practice, but I do not. I am happy to lead the liturgy or concelebrate or simply participate as a member of the congregation. But when I have no better option, I resort to a routine of prayer centered on the Eucharist that I carry with me wherever I go.

I feel much healthier when I sustain a regular rhythm of exercise. During the school year I play basketball with students a couple of times a week; called Monk Hoops by the students, this gives me a chance to blow off steam. In the summer I try most days to jog around the two campus lakes. And I like to walk, especially in cities. When, for whatever reason, I am unable to engage in regular exercise, I feel the difference.

One of the nice things about the rhythm of the academic year is that there are built-in vacation times, although for presidents this does not so much mean time off as a different schedule of events and responsibilities. I figure that I cover 150,000 miles a year in air travel. In connection with our efforts to make Notre Dame more internationally visible, I have traveled with other officers of the university to literally every continent of the world.

Travel goes hand-in-hand with the modern presidency, especially at a national and international university like Notre Dame. One is always subject to the criticism of being gone too much or being a stranger to the campus, and although I believe I have avoided that danger up to now, it is always a hazard worth keeping an eye on. The balancing act is complicated by my desire to be active in national and international organizations and committees. On top of that, Notre Dame has more than two hundred alumni clubs located around the world, and most would like me to visit with some frequency. Despite all this, I try to keep a handle on the pace and extent of my travel.

I believe one of the most important things a president does is decide how to fill up the calendar. Some commitments are unavoidable, but how to use one's discretionary time is a function of the individual's style, years in office, and a variety of factors peculiar to the institution. One of my goals over a multiyear cycle is to meet individually with every faculty member, starting with the full professors and working down the hierarchy. This does not preclude meeting with groups of faculty in other formats, of course, but I enjoy the one-on-one setting, and I think it allows me to establish a distinctive style of administration. I also meet at least once a year with all the middle managers, either in my office or over lunch. I also try to get together with the editors of the student media and other representative student leaders so that we can come to know each other and talk about areas of mutual interest and concern.

I try to celebrate weekend Mass in each of the dorms at least once a year, and I also make myself available to speak in the dorms or help celebrate special dorm occasions. This is also true for professional and graduate student groups and living situations. Some percentage of these events tend to be covered in the student newspaper, which helps me convey the sense of being actively involved in student, staff, and faculty life.

A president has to be open to criticism, and I try to listen to concerns people have with my decisions or my availability or my style. But ultimately a campus leader has to be comfortable with who he or she is, including personal limitations. I tend not to be overly sensitive to criticism, but like everyone else I appreciate receiving a few compliments now and then. I have found in my years as president of Notre Dame that people are very kind in supporting the good things I do and sometimes give me excessive credit for our success as a university. I hope I have learned how to compliment my fellow administrators for jobs well done. All things being equal, I should, like every other president, be ready to take the blame, since I will receive more credit overall than is ever due any individual.

PROTESTS

One tricky challenge that presidents sooner or later have to deal with is sit-ins or other forms of public protest. In my first two terms as president of Notre Dame I had two major sit-ins in the administration building. The first was conducted by a group of minority students who were unhappy about some aspects of race relations at the university and made a series of demands. Although we maintained a security presence in the building during the sit-in, the demonstrators made no effort to enter the president's office. After many hours of negotiating, first with my two assistants and then with a small group of student leaders, we were able to work out a reasonable settlement. No one was arrested, no property was damaged, and both sides could feel they emerged with some portion of their agenda responded to.

As expected, the local television stations and the newspaper were on the scene for all these events and the final resolution. One of the tactics demonstrators use is to try to embarrass the institution with unwanted public exposure. Overall, though, I thought the media reports on that sit-in were fairly well balanced.

The second highly visible demonstration involved anti-abortion demonstrators, many of whom had no connection with Notre Dame. They decided to have a sit-in in a corridor on the first floor of the administration building to protest the fact that we had not allowed them to use Notre Dame property for a meeting. They ignored the fact that they had never made a request for the meeting to the appropriate university officials, dealing only with a small group of our students who also ignored the procedures for scheduling group meetings. Once again we maintained a security presence in the building, although the protesters made no effort to move up to the president's office. The group was relatively nonthreatening, since it included some families and older people.

Our response was to establish a clear set of expectations and then negotiate with the leaders as quickly as possible. Once again, no violence or physical damage was done, and no arrests were made. The publicity on this occasion, primarily because it did not involve very many students, was relatively low key. We held a trump card, because those protesting would have been legally considered trespassers if they had refused to leave the building or the campus.

Other small-scale demonstrations have occurred in my years as president, but colleagues at other institutions profess to be amazed that we have so few. I remember one president of a major state campus saying that he had ten groups demonstrating during a single time span. The protesters this president feared most were animal-rights demonstrators, since they had on some occasions destroyed laboratories and even injured people.

Every president will have his or her own style for dealing with such matters. My fundamental principles are: Be well prepared, avoid direct confrontation, try to initiate a conversation with the leaders as early as possible. So long as everyone understands the ground rules, it is possible to avoid actions that will be more damaging than the publicity that accrues to staged demonstrations. It is important to have both a good security operation and people who know how to handle the publicity in an orderly way.

It is unfortunate that presidents of some institutions need to worry at times about their own or their families' security. On only one occasion in my first two terms as president did someone come to my office who might have been a threat to my well being. Fortunately, my secretary spotted him and called a security guard before he gained admittance. He was arrested after a struggle and eventually brought to trial for trespassing and banned from the campus. For a time after that, we kept a security presence outside my office, partly to calm the fears of employees working in the immediate area of my office. I know presidents who have been physically assaulted or had death threats made against them and their families. In some parts of the world, presidents have been killed by dissidents or the mentally ill.

It is important that security procedures be in place that the major administrators, their secretaries, and campus security all understand thoroughly. If something goes wrong, everyone must know how to handle things. At Notre Dame we have instituted ongoing security in our administration building in the evening hours, not so much because we've had big problems as to create a climate of confidence and security for those who work in the building at night. It is also important to keep the offices of the president and major officers relatively secure because of the sensitive information stored there.

PRESIDENTIAL CHITCHAT

When presidents get together, under whatever auspices, the talk gravitates to certain perennial topics. Two themes are the student newspaper and the faculty senate, or whatever such a group may be called on a given campus. Presidents from similar types of institutions (e.g., private or religiously affiliated or historically black) will share scuttlebutt about trends, crises, or change in leadership.

Among other topics presidents chew over is the importance of having support from the governing board right from the start. A few have lacked that and paid a deep personal price. Another theme is the challenge faced by the spouse of the president in developing a comfortable public role. Related to that is the issue of where one lives. When I was soliciting the advice of other presidents after my election at Notre Dame, the most frequent warning I got was: Don't renovate the president's house in the first year in office. Since I live in a student dormitory, that really wasn't an issue for me, but many presidents have faced accusations of wastefulness and misplaced priorities when the news got out that they were renovating a house that probably needed a lot of work. Maybe the best gift an outgoing president can bestow on a new one is to make sure that such things are attended to before leaving office.

Some very impressive presidents I know seem to possess a combination of talent, energy, and wisdom, while

others have made me wonder how they got their jobs; they
appear to stumble along without ever having an original
idea. Presidential personalities vary widely, from the type
A's who are constantly plugged in to the office through
the telephone or E-mail, to those with a more leisurely
pace or at least a higher level of confidence about their
colleagues in the central administration. Some presidents
are worn down by criticism and carry heavy grudges.
Others possess a level of personal comfort and satisfaction that allows them to maintain an inner core of equa-
nimity and resolution that carries them through even the
worst moments.

I have heard stories about some presidents who have
been involved in criminal behavior, who were addicted to
one form of substance or another, or who have been com-
promised by sexual misconduct. These are a relative few.
The vast majority seem to me to be people of integrity
and good sense; they may not be perfect, but they strive
to live by the standards of professional conduct that go
along with the office.

One of the traditions in the early history of American
higher education was that presidents, many them minis-
ters or priests, were the moral instructors of the campus.
This role involved periodic talks with the student body
about morality. While this style of leadership is no longer
fashionable, I believe that even today presidents can play
such a role to some extent. As a president who is also a
priest, I find that many people, including other presidents,
are interested in what I have to say about matters of religion, ethical standards, or moral practice. In a Catholic
setting, one of the advantages of being a priest/president

is the opportunity to lead the liturgy on institutional occasions in a way that combines both the educational mission of the institution and its religious mission and identity.

BEING THERE

Whenever a disaster or some major tragedy strikes another campus, all presidents want to look in and learn. I
remember a long discussion with John Lombardi, the president of the University of Florida, about how his campus
dealt with a series of off-campus student murders. At Notre
Dame, the most difficult situation I've had to deal with
occurred one icy winter night when a bus carrying our
women's swim team rolled over in blizzard conditions on
the Indiana toll road. Two students were killed, one was
seriously hurt, and many others suffered lesser injuries.

I happened to be in Washington that night, and when
I arrived back on campus the next morning, a security
officer drove me to the scene of the accident, where we
found the bus still upside down beside the highway. We
then hurried to the student health center, where most of
the students were being treated and some of their families
had gathered. Later I went to the hospital and met the most
severely injured student and her parents.

The following day we had a memorial Mass in Sacred
Heart Basilica that was so crowded, many had to listen on
outdoor speakers. I had never before experienced such a
tangible sense of collective mourning and mutual support
as I did that day. Some members of the swim team were in
the congregation, wearing their team overcoats. I have
nothing but compliments for the way everyone pitched

in. It was one of my greatest experiences of the Notre Dame family.

Every campus has its tradition-laden occasions at which the president's presence is absolutely indispensable. For me, this includes our freshman-orientation weekend, when we hold several public events for new students and their parents; home football weekends, which are the times when we host members of our advisory councils and our board of trustees; Junior Parents Weekend, an especially heart-warming interlude in February; and, of course, commencement weekend. I cannot imagine missing any of these; to be absent would suggest that something else is more important, and the office of president has too much symbolic significance to even hint at such a priority.

In addition to these major events, there are other occasions, such as the meetings of our Academic Council or the staff and faculty dinners at the end of the year, which it's imperative for me to be part of. Also important are the Christmas celebrations of campus units. I always give special priority to these parties, and I make sure to spend time with such low-profile groups as the dining hall workers, the maids and janitors, the laundry workers, and the people involved in our campus hotel, our dining facility, and so on. I say a few words of thanks at each event. Although it's impossible to go to every Christmas celebration every year, since some of them conflict with others, I attend as many as feasible.

I try to use my discretionary lunches and dinners as occasions for reaching out to various constituencies. For example, when I can, I like to go out to dinner with groups of students. I also host a dinner for each of the classes I teach.

For many presidents, the cycle of breakfasts, lunches, and dinners can put a great strain on marital and family life. For me, this problem pertains to my relationship with my fellow Holy Cross priests and brothers who live at Notre Dame. We have set aside Sunday and Wednesday as special occasions when everybody tries to be together for prayer and social time and a meal. I endeavor to be as faithful to that schedule as I can, but on other days of the week my presence is rare because of all the demands on my time.

All things being equal, there is a lot to be said for a meal as the setting for both one-on-one and small-group conversations. Sharing food breaks down barriers and fosters relaxed interaction. On the down side, it can be hard to preserve confidentiality or discuss delicate matters in places where others can listen in. Presidents are fortunate if they have a range of dining settings on their campuses for different sets of circumstances.

JOB SATISFACTION

In the end, it is important that a president be happy in the job. I can honestly say I've enjoyed my time as president—it has allowed me to play a significant role in an institution in which I believe deeply. Whatever set of circumstances brought me to the position, I have given it my all. There have been moments that were less than bliss—a few restless nights and occasional regrets about some decision— but overall I can look back and feel good about the things we have been able to achieve together, and about the ways in which I have tried to forge an administrative style that is coherent with my own value system, temperament, and level of energy.

I have met presidents who conveyed a sense of comparable happiness. I have met others who spent most of their time complaining about how bad they had it or how soon retirement would get here. Some presidents no doubt have been asked to do the impossible in failing institutions or have lacked the critical support of their governing board or faculty. The standard complaint of unhappy faculty is to claim that faculty morale "has never been lower"—some observers consider this just a mantra that can be pulled out on selected occasions.

All presidents would like to be loved, or at least appreciated. But I think it is possible for any president to operate with a measure of contentedness and satisfaction. It requires having a relatively clear idea about what they'd like to achieve, and being thankful when the various parts come together.

The presidential path is often circuitous, and the full story of presidential success or leadership will only be told long after most of us have passed from the scene. But I think there are some people whose native gifts and professed desire to make a difference qualify them in a special way to head academic institutions and to be, for at least some period of an institution's history, the right president in the right place at the right moment. All of us hope that that is what will be said about us.

Part Two

Academia and the
Life of the Mind

CHAPTER THREE

Teaching

Teaching in a college or university setting calls for both a deep personal commitment and adherence to certain standards of professional conduct. The teaching faculty are the heart of the modern university, the essential agents of historical continuity. They are entrusted with the primary responsibility for the integrity of the academic mission of the institution.

As an activity, teaching has elements of an art and of a science. Some individuals seem gifted almost from birth with the temperament, energy, discipline, and skills of an effective teacher. Others reach this point only after years of intensive preparation and labor. Perhaps all good teachers were led to the profession by one of their own mentors who by force of example and words of encouragement evoked in the student the necessary spark.

The forms of learning and student-teacher interaction at this particular moment in educational history may be the most diverse and sophisticated that have ever been available. Part of this is driven by computers and other technological devices. But theoretical reflection about learning outcomes and fruitful styles of communication has opened up the possibility that we can be more savvy in organizing our academic structures and in preparing the next generation of college professors.

In this chapter I look at teaching as I have come to understand it through twenty-five years of participation in the profession. I have been blessed with a plethora of great teachers in my own academic preparation. I hope that some of my own students will have positive memories of our time together.

CLASS SIZE

The largest class that I ever taught contained 273 students and met in the library auditorium. It was an introductory course in Christian ethics. The smallest class was a doctoral seminar consisting of four students. There's no doubt in my mind that class size has profound influence on the nature of the student-teacher dynamic.

Very large classes present challenges of a special sort. In the modern university, it is inevitable that some percentage of classes will be taught in large lecture formats, one reason being the limited teaching load enjoyed by faculty in the most prestigious institutions. The rationale is that large lectures for introductory material, which can be relatively routine to teach, free up faculty resources for smaller classes at the advanced undergraduate course level and thus promote effective use of faculty time and energy.

When I was teaching over 270 students in the library auditorium, I used to show up for each session and wonder

just for a moment when the guest of honor would arrive—
I felt like I was going to a distinguished lecture series
rather than to a class I was about to teach. Then I'd come
to my senses and realize that all those people seated in the
auditorium were expecting me to keep them interested and
awake for the next hour or so.

To teach a large lecture class is at least partially to be
an entertainer. Your voice must be properly modulated
and your body constantly in motion, and you need to be
alert for signals of student interest or disinterest. In most
large-class formats the teacher will employ slides, over-
heads, videos, or some other kind of electronic aids to
help concentrate student attention. The DeBartolo classroom building on Notre Dame's campus is a good show-
case for the ways media can be employed to enliven a
large-class lecture session. Yet in the end, the burden falls
upon the professor to be well prepared, engaging, humorous, and concerned about providing personalized instruction to individual students.

In the class I taught in the library auditorium, I was able
to engage the services of a number of graduate students for
fifteen discussion groups that met separately from the lectures. These groups were small enough for students to air
questions about the material and to debate some of the
central issues of the course. Overseeing that many discussion groups is a logistical nightmare, but it was the only
way that I could see to provide opportunities for students
to raise questions and hear from their classmates. Of
course, I welcomed questions in class too, but I was always
aware that if a discussion ran too long we would not cover
the material I thought necessary for that session.

Once a class gets above seventy or eighty, I suspect it

might as well be one hundred or even four hundred, although large sizes do get progressively more impersonal. Almost all megaclasses incorporate some form of discussion outside of the lectures. These days, many professors are learning to take advantage of computer-driven forms of communication: using E-mail, for example, to communicate with their students outside of class, or making class notes available on the campus computer network so that students can concentrate on learning rather than on note-taking in the classroom. For science and other classes with a laboratory component, it is often in the lab sessions that students find a personal form of interaction with graduate students and professors.

My opinion is that we should do everything we can to limit the number of large classes our undergraduate students must take. And it is indispensable that such courses be taught only by faculty who are adept in their preparation and committed to generating enthusiasm among their students. It's worth remembering that some of the most famous teachers in the history of American higher education were known for the large lecture classes that allowed them to affect the intellectual development of countless generations of students.

TUTORIALS AND GRADUATE STUDENTS

In addition to teaching both large and small classes, I have also served as a tutor for students who needed an unavailable course in order to satisfy a requirement. In this role I echoed the normal structure of British higher education, which depends chiefly on tutorial courses. Tutorials put almost all the responsibility on the student to be well prepared for each session. The tutor's role is to recommend readings, to react to the student's oral and written presentations, and to come to some final assessment about the quality of the student's performance.

In America we think of tutorials occasionally under the rubric of directed readings for undergraduate students, but more commonly as the mode of dissertation direction for doctoral students. The relationship between the dissertation director and the directee is perhaps the most crucial one in the course of graduate education. The director often has an instrumental role in suggesting an appropriate dissertation topic. The director also serves as a sounding board, an encourager in times of difficulty or writer's block, and an early-warning system for students who take on more than they can handle, or whose work is effectively second-rate.

My experience suggests that benefits accrue to the dissertation director as well as to the directee in this relationship. It gives the director an opportunity to continue to learn about areas of research beyond his or her native interests or previous work. To serve on the dissertation committee of a young scholar outside of one's field requires coming to the work with an open mind and an interest in drawing connections to one's own field of study. When I have chaired dissertation defenses in fresh fields, I have always found it enjoyable. The chair of the dissertation defense is entrusted with responsibility on behalf of the broader university community to insure that proper procedures are followed and that the student is treated fairly. This includes being aware of unprofessional rivalries on the committee or inadequate preparation in the committee's reading of the text that might affect the ultimate decision.

One of the biggest complaints heard about dissertation directors is the sluggishness with which they sometimes respond to their students' work. In the midst of a busy semester, thousands of things clamor for the director's attention and concern. The farther away from the directee's campus the director must be, the greater the temptation to shunt off the next reading of the material presented until a more convenient time. No one can tell a director, amid his or her multiple responsibilities, how promptly to respond to a directee, but persistently putting off a reading and response until a semester break or the summer months can prolong the directee's completion for one or more years. The pursuit of a doctorate inevitably involves delayed gratification and persistence in the task, to be sure, but it is unfair to let a directee dangle for months.

TEACHING BY CASE

No format for education is perfect, and all class sizes have both advantages and disadvantages. In the end, for undergraduate students I favor a few large classes, many medium to small classes, and a few integrated seminars. The majority of classes taught to undergraduates at a school like Notre Dame are in the thirty-five to one hundred range. In classes of this size it is possible both to cover sufficient material in the lectures and also to allow some discussion, either with the whole class or in smaller groupings within the class.

Because many of the courses I taught when I was a full-time faculty member in the theology department were in the area of ethics, I found that the use of well chosen and representative cases was a good device. I would take a class of, say, fifty students and have them gather in groups of ten to discuss a case for five to ten minutes, then have them share a summary of their conclusions. This was easier to pull off in the Tuesday/Thursday seventy-five-minute class sequence than in the Monday/Wednesday/Friday fifty-minute classes. Nevertheless, I found a way of using cases in both kinds of sessions.

I believe that effective lecturing draws upon one's native gifts as well as thoughtful preparation and honest feedback. Some professors, by dint of personality and special gifts, could teach any kind of content and be interesting; others need to work constantly on their lecturing style and content. Most professors come out of graduate school afraid that they will run out of material too quickly in the semester, and so over prepare. With a year or two of experience under their belts, disciplined and motivated professors gain a feel for how much content can be treated in a semester and what percentage of each class session must contribute to that goal.

I favor using outside readings to supplement the content of lectures rather than the other way around. This approach allows the course to have a broader perspective and to cover a wider range of issues than is possible when the lectures supplement the readings. I realize, of course, that some fields of study best employ survey books or other material that forms the main content of the class. The role of the teacher then is to clarify the texts and help students attain confidence in comprehending the material.

In my lectures in theology and ethics, I tend to take nothing for granted. With undergraduate students I try to introduce not only a feel for the issues but also a way of thinking about them, since even the brightest students are often methodologically unsophisticated. I also possess a particularly historical orientation, so I believe that learning the history of reflection on a topic or issue is a good way to approach the contemporary debate. To talk about a Christian theology of marriage, for example, it is important to ground students in the biblical material and in the evolution of theological reflection on the subject through the centuries. This also allows for covering differences among the Christian denominations with regard to the theology of marriage.

The closer one comes to the contemporary problematic, the more necessary it is to be cross-disciplinary. To think about a contemporary Christian theology of marriage is to take into account psychological, sociological, anthropological, legal, and other perspectives on the same reality. Why do contemporary Western people view arranged marriages as repugnant? To discover that this form of matchmaking has prevailed through much of human history and continues to be the dominant mode in some cultures even today is to be open to a fresh set of perspectives. To think theologically about Christian marriage in the broader context is to take up questions about the having of children, about the permanence of the bond, and about the different kinds of support systems that have prevailed in past cultures. A good lecturer gets the students thinking in creative and challenging ways. The readings chosen for the course can then expand the student's perspective.

SEMINARS

For the last eleven years I have been teaching first-year undergraduates a seminar whose content covers eight novels and two movies. I assign ten papers of two to three pages each and a final paper of five to seven pages that is intended to give the class a chance to synthesize the semester's material. We meet in the president's conference room in the Main Building once a week for two and a half hours, with a short break in the middle. I limit the class to eighteen students. I don't control who gets in the class, but I do ask the First Year of Studies staff to assign me as diverse a group by background as they can provide. Normally, half the students are male and half are female. They represent a cross section of ethnic and racial backgrounds, and I usually have several international students among them. I never use the same books or movies from one year to the next, and this allows me to explore a wide range of material. The general theme of the course through the years has been exposure to other cultures and ways of life. I choose each of the books and movies because it is set in another country, culture, or historical period.

I expect students to come to every class, to be well prepared, and to speak up in class. I spend an introductory session trying to learn as much as I can about each student; I have them interview one another and then introduce the person to the left or right. I tell them I expect them to know all the other names by the end of the class. My aim is to establish as personal and intimate a conversation as one can expect from students in their first year of college. By the end of the semester, even the shy ones are fairly prepared to speak out.

The teacher of a seminar must both calm down the vociferous students and engage those who are hesitant. Students find it tempting not to listen to their classmates but to spend class time preparing what they will say when it is their turn. As the semester goes on, I try to let the students themselves direct the flow of conversation more and more. I even invite some of them to be discussion leaders.

The great advantage of the seminar format is that it encourages maximum student participation. This allows them to test ideas, be surprised by peer insights into familiar material, and gain confidence that they have something to say. The chief danger of the seminar approach is that it may end up being nothing more than shared ignorance, or else may so diverge from the content of the text that it becomes simply an encounter group. I try to avoid those pitfalls by choosing interesting, provocative material, and then trying to ensure that we attend to basic themes, significant culture factors, and the artistry of the writer or film director. I also encourage students to draw connections between what we are talking about in class and their own lives and experiences. For example, it is inevitable in the course of the semester that we will touch on questions of male-female relations, of the notion of family, of the dilemmas of the poor and marginalized, of the influence of religion, of the nature of education, and many other foundational topics.

Having students write relatively short papers each week is a good exercise, I have found; not only does it force them to finish the material ahead of time, but it also forces them to identify what they think are the important dimensions of the material. I don't tell them what to write about, but I try to get them to draw a connection between the overall work and the particular details that allow the story to be interesting and worth reviewing. I stress that what I look for most of all in their papers is content rather than form. The students I get are reasonably good writers, but their big challenge is to develop confidence that they have something worthwhile to say. The worst of my students have been decent, and the best have been extraordinary.

One advantage of a diverse class is that the students embody in their own backgrounds the kind of things we talk about in class. When the group is diverse enough, especially in appearance, no one student has to represent a particular group's perspective. That frees everyone to respond to their classmates simply as individuals. Although I don't think all classes need to be so manifestly diverse, it does offer a great opportunity for students from fairly homogeneous backgrounds to experience the company of others who are different from themselves.

PERSONALIZING THE LEARNING
RELATIONSHIP

Two facets of my teaching approach, I believe, deserve emulation. The first is that I meet with each of my students individually for about half an hour sometime during the semester. One criticism of faculty today in many institutions is their unavailability outside the classroom. Even when faculty members post office hours, students sometimes find that they are either not reliably there, or they appear sufficiently bothered when a student shows up that word gets around that they really don't mean it when they say they're available.

Personal interviews with students help solidify a relationship between student and teacher. My tendency is to spend most of the time in these conferences exploring the student's background and previous educational experience rather than simply focusing on the quality of his or her class performance. I do try to give feedback, of course, but only after students have had a chance to talk about themselves in a nonthreatening conversation. It is amazing how frank and revealing students can be in these interviews. Still, I make sure that I do not push the boundary of the relationship. To the students in my class, I am their teacher; if they want a relationship with me as a priest or counselor as well, then they need to solicit that on their own initiative.

The second technique I strongly advocate is to hold a class dinner at the end of the semester. Because of my present administrative role, I have the wherewithal to act as dinner host in a university setting that is somewhat apart from where the students live. Because the meal is provided by dining hall services, we can simply be together and have a good time. After we eat, I usually have them discuss what they have learned during the course, academically or otherwise. Then we play some kind of competitive table game such as Scattergories or Pictionary. By the end of the games they are usually laughing and screaming at one another, releasing some of the pent-up energy that inevitably builds toward the end of a semester.

I know that many faculty try to do something social with their students, either in one large group or in smaller units. I don't think any single thing is more conducive to cementing the bonds that develop over the course of a semester.

The Pain of Grading

Perhaps the most unpleasant aspect of being a teacher is having to give exams or in some other way evaluate students. In designing the structure of a class, one of the most significant choices to be made is dividing up the semester's work in a way that permits fair evaluation of student performance. When it comes to doctoral students, I have found that a combination of in-class discussions and a final paper provides a pretty reliable sense of a the student's ability and performance. It is hard for the slacker to hide or the incompetent to pull off the impossible.

Yet it is difficult in a relatively small class of doctoral students to assign grades. It is the combination of grades achieved in such classes over the course of two or three years of class work that gives the faculty as a whole a sense of the reasonable probability that the student will be able to pass comprehensives and complete a good dissertation. But too often inflated grades, given by individual professors with all the good will in the world, will deny the department a reliable assessment of the individual's ability and performance. To receive less than a B in a doctoral course is effectively to fail. But the difference between an A and a B can make all the difference in one's career prospects.

Evaluating performance is particularly challenging with undergraduates, and the biggest dilemma is choosing an appropriate testing format. For large classes it seems easier to utilize computer-generated multiple-choice or true-and-false questions. For faculty, this approach means that most of their effort goes into structuring the questions and a small amount into reviewing the answers. The problem with this approach, first of all, is that it requires the professor to have confidence that both probability theory and the nature of the material can allow for a fair appraisal to take place in a machine-corrected format. Secondly, such tests do not allow partial credit to be given when only a small mistake keeps a student from having the right answer. In disciplines that think of themselves as objective, this may be an attractive way of testing—you are either right or wrong, and there's no in-between. The kinds of material that I have been teaching, however, do not allow for this level of certainty.

I am much more interested in subtlety and style of argumentation, and in drawing connections, than I am in the so-called objective answer. Therefore, in my undergraduate classes I employ multiple modes of testing, usually combining essay exams with short definitions of terms and fill-in-the-blank questions or other ways of integrating the concrete and specific with more general forms of analysis. I always have my students write one or more papers to supplement what they do on written tests. The combination of papers plus tests gives me a more valid assessment of the individual student.

In the end, every testing scheme is limited. At best, tests are both prods to encourage students to learn and a means of preserving fairness in differentiating students who work hard from those who do not. They also provide a means by which faculty can recommend, or not, students for further educational programs. Like most professors, I hate grading, but I believe it to be an inevitable part of professorial responsibilities.

ATTENDANCE

In an ideal world, students would go to class or lab or performance session solely out of a desire to learn. But in the real world, where university faculties establish policies that regulate student academic life, attendance policy is one area about which there is some variation in practice.

At Notre Dame, we consider it the professor's responsibility in the introductory class session to explain his or her expectations. Some professors, often by reputation, convey a sense that it makes no difference whether or not a student makes up missed classes, particularly in the large-class lecture format. Generally, the smaller the class, the higher the expectations all around that the student be there regularly.

It is my deep conviction that students should attend class consistently and regularly. In my first-year seminar, I expect all my students to be at every class unless there are serious extenuating circumstances. I prefer to argue that if students as a group find a particular class unexciting and unfulfilling, it is up to the university community to do something about it.

In the end, I feel about students who miss my classes the way I do about those who miss Masses or parties that I host or any other social occasion. If someone is missing, it concerns me. If they are missing on a regular basis, I will try to find out why.

JUDGING THE JUDGES

One of the most vexing issues in higher education is how to evaluate the quality of teaching. If teaching is both an art and science, as I believe it is, then some people are naturally gifted as teachers. But gifted or not, it is possible to learn the rudiments of the craft and, with proper feedback, to improve one's teaching competency. Notre Dame's Kaneb Center for Teaching, directed by Professor Barbara Walvoord, is a most welcome addition to the campus learning environment. Professor Walvoord, an expert on pedagogy, is well versed in the methodologies of teaching and possesses great experience, energy, and enthusiasm. It was gratifying to observe how many of our faculty quickly sought out her services when the center was established.

One body of opinion suggests that it's virtually impossible to evaluate teaching fairly because no consensus exists concerning the qualities that make a teacher good. Anecdotal evidence is presented to celebrate such a wide variety of teaching styles and personality types that, it is argued, generalizing is impossible. Most institutions like Notre Dame employ an end-of-the-semester form on which students evaluate the teachers in each of their courses. Students answer twenty or thirty questions related to the teaching quality and the course content, and these answers are tallied numerically so that comparisons may be studied from semester to semester. When faculty are up for promotion decisions, summaries of their student evaluations are an integral part of the packet made available to those involved in the evaluation process.

Most people believe that these teacher evaluation forms, along with the oral reputation each teacher accumulates, make it easy to separate out those faculty members who stand at either end of the distribution curve—that is, the very best and the very worst. If patterns of excellence or underperformance prevail over time, then the decision about promotion is easy. Even though promotion decisions involve more than just teaching, that facet of the faculty member's activity should be a significant part of the final determination.

The real difficulty with the evaluation form is what to make of those who stand in the middle of the pack. It is not unusual for faculty to do better in certain class sizes than in others, or to flourish with some but not all content. Some faculty excel in large classes; others find them difficult. Some faculty are outstanding dissertation directors who win the admiration of their graduate students but don't do well in undergraduate courses. Some faculty

develop a popular following that tends to glamorize their
reputation with subsequent generations of students.

But what is an evaluator to make of wide variations in
teaching reports from one semester to another? What
about the faculty member who starts haltingly but shows
signs of improvement around the time that the tenure or
promotion decision must be made—yet is still not above
the mean for the department, college, or university? It is
in these situations that prudential judgment is required.

Another thorny question in discussions about the evaluation of teaching is whether or not peer visits should be an
integral part of the process. Some colleges at Notre
Dame have institutionalized regular visitation by departmental colleagues to classes taught by teachers who are
up for promotion. This is usually done with advance notice and with multiple visitors participating. Others of
our colleges resist this practice; they seem to feel visita-
tions skew the teaching process or create artificial classroom conditions that make fair evaluation impossible.

I find it disappointing that peer visitation is not accepted
across the university landscape. How can faculty colleagues
review the teaching skills of a colleague whom they have
never seen teaching? What is offensive about being given
the opportunity to display one's skills in a real-life teaching situation? Surely having a faculty member present a
paper to faculty colleagues at a colloquium—a practice
often resorted to in the evaluation process—is hardly the
same thing as performing in the classroom. Perhaps the
best way to think about this matter is to put oneself in the
place of the father or mother of a student. From that vantage point, is the faculty member the kind of skilled pro-

fessional that students have the right to expect? And how is one to determine that?

The answer, I believe, is that a combination of student evaluation of faculty plus peer review provides the foundation of a proper evaluation of teaching. And these gauges should be supplemented by annual reviews from the departmental chair and/or dean. Such reviews should be based upon a self-evaluation by the faculty member. Deficiencies in teaching should be pointed out, and efforts to improve should be initiated. If the teacher receives this sort of annual feedback, then there is explicit fairness in the system.

It is crucial for universities to commit institutionally to the honest evaluation of teaching. The other criteria upon which faculty promotion decisions are based—research in one's discipline and service to the university and community—seem at face value to be more objective and easier to quantify. That poses the danger, through academic neglect or because of the inability to achieve a consensus about teaching criteria, of creating a situation where teaching skill simply doesn't count for much. To reach such a point would be tragic for our students and terrible for our institutions, and we must not allow it to happen.

At a minimum, we should expect faculty to be well prepared, deeply committed to students, open to feedback from whatever source, interested in the teaching styles and techniques of their peers, freely available to students outside the classroom, and fair in their evaluation of student performance. I'm convinced that the vast majority of faculty, at Notre Dame and elsewhere, exhibit these qualities. But like all professionals, we need to recognize the temptations we face collectively and be courageous in doing the right thing for the right reason.

MEMORABLE TEACHERS

This discussion of teaching would be incomplete without a representative sampling of the teachers who have made a profound difference in my own life. Father John Dunne, C.S.C., is one.

When I first met John in my last semester as a Notre Dame undergraduate, he already possessed legendary status in my peer culture. During my semester with him, what I came to admire most were his bubbly personality, his simplicity, and his great openness of mind and spirit. He was my fourth theology professor at Notre Dame but the first one to convince me that theology not only could be interesting but could also be the work of a lifetime for me. John delivered his lectures without using a note. He made reference to figures across all the disciplines but focused on issues that we seniors thought were what college was all about. He convinced us that we could pass over into the world view of others, including others who were hostile to religion, and pass back again into our own perspective changed for the better. He broadened our horizons and helped us see life in more holistic terms than we had been accustomed to. He modeled how a believer in Jesus could also be a respector of other religious traditions and ways of life. I subsequently had John for other courses, and I've read many of his books. He represents for me the teacher who was challenging, inspiring, and encouraging.

Another memorable teacher I had as an undergraduate was Robert Turley, who taught philosophy. Bob was a relatively young man who introduced us to a wide range of thinkers such as Darwin, Marx, and Freud. Because he seemed so sensible and sane, we took him at his word when he suggested that we could become familiar with these intellectuals without necessarily risking our faith or self-confidence. Bob was not a propagandist or an advocate, but rather a scholar who tried to engage us with the ideas of others.

A third was Edward Cronin, whom I had for two Great Books seminars. We started in the Greco-Roman period and read the great works of the Western world up into the modern era. Ed was an avuncular figure who reminded me of the television image of Walter Cronkite. He used to bring a pipe to class, and he would spend most of the period trying to light it. It was a delightful prop that gave him an appearance of what we imagined a true intellectual to look like. Ed had his own system of writing, to which he expected his students to conform. We used to get more red markings back on our papers than the original black compositions that we contributed. But the combination of classroom interaction and the response to our papers showed us that Ed Cronin took us seriously. He used to delight in having in his classes a large percentage of student athletes who came from poor backgrounds. He saw it as a challenge to open up that kind of blue-collar student to the exciting world of literature and ideas.

Also impressive was Donald Costello of the English department. One of the first professors at Notre Dame who brought cinema into the classroom, Don had us reading fiction, viewing plays, and being exposed to some of the avant-garde films from European directors of the day. What I liked about his classes was his use of more than one kind of material to hold our attention. He convinced us that reading and viewing—that is, viewing plays and films—were akin in the demands they made on the reader/viewer, and that both verbal and visual images, through the intervention of the creative artist, construct worlds that are delightful and aesthetically pleasing.

The last professor I'll mention is Joseph F. X. Brennan of the English department. Joe loved words and was one of the most articulate teachers I ever had. I remember him complaining, many years later, that he was a slow reader, but that never got in the way of his analysis of the way form contributes to content in creative work. Joe stimulated my interest in etymology and in the beautiful ways in which words can affect the heart and spirit. I had him for four courses, two as an undergraduate and two as a graduate student. I never tired of listening to him speak, and I was greatly affected by his love of literature.

NEGATIVE IMAGES

Not all teachers are models of the calling. Here are a few negative images of teachers, especially as filtered by the peer culture of the professoriat.

The performer: On any campus one finds a certain number of professors who are extremely popular with students and have a highly developed public persona. Students like to get into their classes, and by word of mouth they attract continual acclaim. Often these professors teach large lecture classes and therefore have access to a significant number of students through the years. These "performers," however, are often viewed by colleagues as all form and no substance. They are thought to pander to the masses, to play to the youth culture, to offer pabulum when real meat is called for.

Sometimes such faculty members focus on materials that are especially interesting to young adults, making continual reference to music or films or dance or other aspects of youth culture and entertainment. Generally, faculty performers are glib, articulate, witty, and personable. Some spend huge amounts of time with students outside the classroom, especially in social situations. In some cases, they may hang out at student-oriented establishments.

Recognizing that there can be a certain amount of jealousy in colleague evaluations of faculty performers, there is nonetheless a legitimate concern about the need for substance in class content, about the necessity of preserving a professional distance in one's interaction with young people, and about the nature of one's interaction with fellow professors in the same academic unit. All faculty may have a bit of performer in them, or might be performance-oriented at some times in their academic career. There is nothing wrong with occasionally playing to the crowd or relishing popularity. But in the end, the temptation is for a faculty member to become simply an actor playing a role and not a thoughtful, mature professional person.

The guru: Some faculty, through force of personality or the attractiveness of either their field of study or their own history, become critically influential in the lives of some percentage of their students, who view the guru as the purveyor of wisdom, the provider of a philosophy of life, and the instructor in techniques for self-realization and fulfillment. Those faculty who attain guru status may do so simply by the brilliance of their minds or the creative power that they exercise.

To win a Nobel Prize or a Pulitzer, or to be admitted to one of the national honorary societies for faculty, attracts a significant amount of attention not only to oneself but also to one's department, college, or university. There is often a fair amount of ego invested in getting to that point, and the temptation then is to think of oneself as universally wise and competent. Thus we find world-class mathematicians acting like philosophers and engineers redesigning foreign policy. I'm not suggesting that faculty should be disqualified by their breadth of interests, but rather warning that people sometimes pay attention to a famous faculty member's words because of his or her competence in a field that is in reality quite limited.

At the graduate level, the faculty guru tends to dominate a department or to be in rivalry with a competitive guru. This complicates life for graduate students, who feel forced to make decisions about which camp they will belong to, choices that can make a tremendous difference in their future careers. At the undergraduate level, student disciples hover around a faculty guru, treating him or her as a personal counselor or group adviser and seeking a sign of favor or a special moment of insight.

The notion of a teaching guru is fraught with difficulty. It too easily confuses the multiple roles that a faculty member might play in a student's life. It can freeze-frame a student at a certain level of development and prevent her or him from developing a sense of self or clarifying personal values and goals. All faculty might harbor the desire to be thought wise by their students, but the self-knowledge that is an integral part of wisdom would suggest that this role ought to be a rare one, and usually consigned to faculty who are right in age and mature enough to handle it.

The robot: Perhaps the clearest case of faculty ineptitude is the teacher who totally lacks any overt commitment to the calling. Such faculty may be decently knowledgeable about their subject, but they put little effort into learning proper techniques of communication or engaging their students with enthusiasm or humor. The stereotypical example of the robot teacher is the person who employs the same set of notes semester after semester, with almost no variance. Outside of the United States, one might get away with simply reading old notes word for word, year after year, but in this country teaching expectations make such behavior totally unacceptable.

The robot teacher is all head and no heart or spirit. He or she accepts the old *Dragnet* theme, "just the facts." Yet the very art of learning includes interpretation of material and a willingness to recognize competing methodological perspectives and reasonable areas of disagreement. The robot may never miss a day of class, but very early in the semester the students, if they can, will begin voting with their feet by transferring out of the course. If the professor is a quirky grader in addition to being uninteresting, then the exodus will be even more pronounced.

To sum up, the professor as performer errs by trying too hard to please. The professor as guru confuses the role of academic expert with that of personal adviser or religious mentor. The professor as robot satisfies the minimum requirements of the job without recognizing the need for stimulation and engagement of a more profound sort.

SETTING THE CULTURE

The distribution of teaching responsibilities within an academic department is something of an art. Like it or not, the professoriat is a hierarchical society, and the great dividing line lies between those who are tenured and those who are not. Among the tenured, higher acclaim and influence are accorded to full professors and even more to those who hold chairs. The value set of any department is established by the approximately two-thirds of the faculty who are tenured; they send the signals to junior faculty about what standards of expectation will be in place when their time comes to be evaluated for promotion and tenure.

Part of passing on the heritage is done orally, in statements by the appropriate committees or the department chair. But it is also embedded in the perceived priorities of the senior faculty themselves. When full professors teach first-year undergraduates, then that is seen as a priority; when senior professors display sufficient responsibility to pass along a favored course to serve the common good, everyone notices. Exhortations by presidents, provosts, and deans can have some influence, but they are nowhere near as important as the messages passed on by senior faculty to their junior colleagues.

One of the primary responsibilities of the departmental chair is to see that the overall teaching responsibilities of the department are fairly distributed. This requires taking into account who will be on leave during a given semester, what foundational courses simply have to be taught, and how much flexibility exists in allowing faculty members to offer specialized courses. A healthy department involves sufficient give and take so that students have access to the courses they need. Both undergraduates and graduates are taken fully into account. Normally, it is unacceptable to force a faculty member on a group of students when that teacher is known not to be effective in a given teaching format. Thus large lecture classes and introductory courses should not be assigned to faculty who are less than adept in this mode of instruction, if it can be avoided.

No professor should be expected to direct an inordinate number of doctoral dissertations. No matter how attractive the professor, this is not good for either the faculty member or his or her students. Departmental administrative and counseling responsibilities should also be brought into the equation. And, needless to say, not everyone can teach at a preferred hour or in a favored weekly sequence. As long as the chair is consistent and fair in making decisions, the typical faculty member will accept the call to sacrifice when it comes.

Of considerable importance to the health of an academic department is the mentoring of junior faculty by senior professors, particularly in regard to teaching. One of the most helpful initiatives a department can take when a new faculty member joins its ranks is to make sure that the newcomer is assigned a senior faculty member as a mentor. If the department is large enough, the assignment will take place within a subspecialty. Such personalized initiation into a departmental culture is a good way to make new faculty feel comfortable about with the way things are done in a given institutional setting.

An integral part of the conversation between junior faculty member and senior mentor should be expectations about teaching. These conversations might range across a variety of topics, including what the normal number of books or other materials assigned to a given class may be, what the expected number of tests or papers is, how severe the grading tradition is, and so on. That still leaves the prerogative with the individual junior faculty member to make choices about his or her way of doing things, but at least the newcomer will not act out of naïveté about the traditions of the academic unit. One of the greatest fears junior faculty have is that they will receive unnecessarily low student evaluations when they begin teaching because they may stray too far from the norm. If a faculty member wants to develop a reputation as a tough grader, that is up to him or her. But it's important to make that decision on the basis of all the available evidence.

Another topic capable of touching off vigorous debate on university campuses is team teaching. When it comes to the efficient use of faculty resources, it does not seem at first glance that team teaching should claim a high priority in the modern academy. With many faculty in research universities teaching reduced loads, it goes against the grain to suggest that two or more faculty members team up to offer a single course. Nevertheless, there are good arguments for this style of teaching.

Early in my career at Notre Dame, I team-taught a course with the Protestant ethicist Stanley Hauerwas. The two of us were interested in similar kinds of issues but had much different perspectives. In the course of the semester we were able to expose our students to the kind of informed discussion that we hoped they might someday engage in themselves. I think they found it fascinating to discover that faculty members could disagree extensively, yet still have a good working relationship. That's one kind of team-teaching model.

Another is to have people from different disciplines teach materials that have an intersecting intellectual focus. Thus a biologist and a philosopher might be interested in questions related to environmental ethics. An architect, a political scientist, and an economist might join to teach a course on urban planning, exploring all the ramifications of public policy in this regard. A lawyer and a theologian might examine questions relating to death, dying, and medical ethics. In these cases, combining faculty with different training and different fields of expertise can offer a lively and stimulating model of the kind of exchange one would hope would exist among the broader citizenry.

The logistics of team-taught courses can be expensive and complex. But many faculty will attest from experience that such courses can be the most enjoyable form of teaching for both faculty and students. One of the roles that multidisciplinary centers and institutes play in the life of a university is to promote this sort of interaction, not only in the form of classes but also in combined research projects and in colloquia and conferences.

THE REWARDS OF TEACHING

In their best moments, faculty in higher education recognize the rare privilege that they enjoy. They get paid for doing something close to their heart's desire. The responsibility for teaching a course taps into years of formal preparation, previous experience of academic interaction, and a whole range of personal interests and related competencies. The dedicated teacher is forced to be a lifelong learner, for nothing is less exciting than formulaic instruction or unabsorbed theories. It is only when the professor can convey some portion of the excitement of discovery and the thrill of mastery that a similar dynamic can be set off in the student.

One of the mysteries of the learning environment is that the teacher can never be certain who in the assembly of students entrusted to his or her care will be the most personally affected. The normal array of testing vehicles may give us some clues, but in the end each of us is only part of a process, loosely organized as it sometimes seems to be. If we cannot guarantee the success of our efforts, neither can we shirk the obligation to do our very best. What we have first learned ourselves, we must pass on as masterfully as we can. And in the process of doing so, we may sometimes bear good fruit beyond our wildest imagining.

CHAPTER FOUR

Research and Scholarship

Of the three main professorial responsibilities in the modern American university—teaching, research, and service—the least familiar to those outside the academy is scholarly research. Many people pursue teaching as a profession or can imagine doing so, and even more have engaged in some kind of service. Service in the academy can range from participation on departmental, collegiate, or university committees to leadership in learned societies to generous involvement in organizations with a civic, religious, or social amelioration purpose. But the relative isolation and discipline required for research and scholarship is uniquely transmitted from one generation to the next by the tradition and examples passed along in graduate school and beyond.

Since neither of my parents and almost none of my relatives went to college, I grew up with no firsthand acquaintance with scholarship as a way of spending a lifetime. I was an avid reader, however, and that surely was one wellspring for my insatiable desire to know more about areas I found interesting. During my undergraduate days at Notre Dame I managed to amass a fairly sizable paperback library, mostly literature. Implicit in accumulating a personal library is the presumption that one might want to return to books previously read, or perhaps to explore the connections among several works by the same author. My library also made it possible for me to lend books I enjoyed to fellow students. To be in the company of other burgeoning scholars amassing their own libraries is to begin an ongoing conversation about things that touch us in more than perfunctory fashion.

At Notre Dame I also took my introductory steps into the world of high culture, attending concerts and plays and making occasional visits to an art gallery or museum. Most of these forays were unconnected to a class assignment. As I grew older, I came to see these activities as part of what an educated person does to gain a broader background and a more comfortable familiarity with works considered "great."

I was aware that I had a fairly high IQ, and I began to believe that I might possesses some God-given academic ability that was not dependent on family upbringing or socioeconomic circumstances. Over time, I gained confidence in my ability to master new fields of study and to hold my own in analyzing and debating complex questions. This confidence probably started in the bull sessions that are a part of undergraduate life.

Yet I was both attracted and put off by those coteries of students, sometimes sharing a common major, who fancied themselves "intellectuals" but often seemed pretentious and arty. Although I was an English major, I never gravitated toward that inner circle of majors who exuded an attitude of superiority. Perhaps because I was also a jock, I learned to navigate multiple worlds simultaneously, accentuating one side of my personality with one group and another side in a different social configuration.

Very early on in the seminary I began to think in vocational terms about focused kinds of ministry. The dominant image I entertained in those days placed me in a university setting as a priest, teacher, scholar, and minister. After my candidate year, when I studied philosophy and Latin and took a graduate class or two in English on my own initiative, I moved on to the novitiate where there were no formal classes for credit. But when I returned to Notre Dame, I continued my pursuit of a master's degree in English along with my philosophy and Latin studies, and by the time I was ordained in 1970 I had completed both a master's in English and a master's in theology. My grades were outstanding and I had very high scores on the graduate record exams.

As I pondered what might come after ordination, I sought advice from priest-scholars on the Notre Dame faculty. Initially I had thought to pursue a doctorate in the field called "theology and literature," a program available only at the University of Chicago and a few other places. But the advice I got, in retrospect very helpful, was that neither theologians nor literature faculty would give much credence to somebody with that mixture. When the time finally came to decide what subspecialty of theology to pursue, by a process of elimination I felt I would be happiest pursuing a degree in Christian ethics.

I applied to five schools, was accepted at three, and chose Vanderbilt University for several reasons: I felt the Vanderbilt program had a strong reputation, I was offered a very good financial package, and Nashville was far enough away from Notre Dame not to present ongoing temptation to make frequent visits to the campus. I spent three years in residence at Vanderbilt and another year and a half finishing my dissertation after I returned to Notre Dame.

I remember vividly my first year at Vanderbilt. I was living with Ollie Williams—another Holy Cross priest studying at Vanderbilt for his doctorate in theology. This was an advantage, since I was not entirely on my own. I made every effort to get to know my fellow students in the ethics program and to begin the long process of integrating myself into the world of graduate education. The divinity school at Vanderbilt seemed much friendlier than at other schools I had heard about. The faculty worked closely with the students, and there was very little dog-eat-dog competition. Many of us felt a bit at sea for a while, since we were expected to define our own extra-reading program and to begin thinking about a dissertation topic and about which faculty members we might work with on the dissertation.

The first great challenge for me was the absence in the curriculum of an organized introduction to the field of Christian ethics. The courses we took gave us bits and pieces of background, but the faculty had an overly narrow perspective on the courses they taught from semester to semester. I vividly remember an angry meeting in the second semester of my first year between graduate students in ethics and the ethics faculty. The students were demanding a one- or two-semester, broad-based, historically grounded introduction to Christian ethics; they were also reacting against some of the research interests of the faculty that seemed to have been foisted upon them. I do not recall many concrete results from that discussion, but I can say that since joining the faculty at Notre Dame I have always tried to provide a historical introduction to Christian ethics in courses I've taught at the graduate level.

For many graduate students, the first exposure to scholarly activity comes in writing course papers. In most Ph.D. classes there are no tests, and the whole grade depends upon the quality of a single paper. This takes some getting used to, but it also bestows freedom to spend one's time outside of class as one wishes. By my second year of course work, I had a much better sense of what I wanted to be reading and a surer capacity for making connections between one course and another. In my third year I spent much of my time working my way through extensive reading lists to prepare for comprehensive exams and to develop a dissertation proposal.

Perhaps never again in my life will I feel such a sense of accomplishment as I felt that year. I read constantly, took copious notes, then reorganized the notes so that by the time I took the comprehensive exams, I was developing a sense of confidence and comprehensiveness in my field. I was also still cultivating my personal library, which by then included as many of the works of the central figures in Christian ethics, Catholic and Protestant, as I could come by. I had also become knowledgeable about the major journals in my field and could tick off influential figures and where they stood within the spectrum of opinion.

There is no substitute that I can imagine for the hard

work and endless hours of reading, synthesis, and reflection that prepared me for my comprehensives and dissertation. When I began teaching at Notre Dame, I drew constantly from the material I had covered during this time, and the intricate outlines I had prepared on the basis of that reading. Because I have always had an ability to reduce large bodies of material into finer and more precise units, I could take a two hundred- or three hundred-page book and, in a relatively compact way, replay the central ideas, terminological distinctions, and important data. It never bothered me, at least at that stage of my life, that some people seemed to be able to do this all in their head, while my approach was more plodding.

During the time I was working on my dissertation, I reverted to a more focused expenditure of energy and time. I have gone in my life from wide-ranging reading, with no obvious limits of interest or perspective, to highly focused and analytical concentration on a relatively limited amount of material. I could not have successfully engaged in the second without having experienced the first.

By the time I had finished my Ph.D., five years after my ordination, I felt I was legitimately a scholar-in-the-making. I had passed muster, at least from the point of view of my faculty mentors. When I was hired as an assistant professor at Notre Dame, I knew I was entering a profession that carried with it responsibilities for ongoing research and writing that would be valuable not only for their own sake but also to make me a more effective teacher—and, in my case, preacher and counselor. In retrospect, none of this seems predestined; it stemmed from a series of opportunities that were offered to me. I feel fortunate indeed to have had the opportunity to pursue research and scholarship at a major American university.

CHANGING EXPECTATIONS

As any grade school or high school teacher can testify from firsthand experience, teaching, all by itself, can be all-consuming. Giving proper attention to such matters as class preparation, the formation of appropriate testing devices, correcting assignments, assigning grades, and meeting with students and parents is a full-time occupation—not to mention departmental meetings, extracurricular activity supervision, or continuing education events.

Through much of the history of American higher education, the teaching demands placed upon faculty were intensive. When I was a student at Notre Dame in the early sixties, the typical teaching load was four courses a semester, and the faculty, at least in the College of Arts and Letters, very seldom had individual offices and had to meet with students in open rooms shared with several other colleagues. It was difficult to have time or sufficient independence in one's schedule to be very active in scholarly research.

Even back in the nineteenth century, I'm certain, there were scholars in the elite American institutions who compared in ability and output to scholars in the finest European universities. But that was atypical and not expected, even in the Ivy League institutions. Then, in the early part of the twentieth century, a new kind of American university began to emerge under the influence of the German university model. Institutions like Johns Hopkins, the University of Chicago, Massachusetts Institute of Technology, and Washington University in St. Louis were developed primarily as graduate institutions with heavy orientation toward research.

An even more dramatic and influential change grew out of the Second World War. During that conflict, many American universities were mobilized as part of the war effort—the Manhattan Project at the University of Chicago, for instance, drew physicists and scientists from a wide variety of institutions—and that set a pattern for heavy government subsidies for research within universities. After the war, the federal government, through a number of federal entities, effectively became a gigantic source of research dollars, particularly in science and engineering. The National Science Foundation, the National Institutes of Health, and other programs under the auspices of the Department of Defense, the Department of Agriculture, the Department of Labor, and similar agencies developed a system of peer review for the distribution of the millions of dollars to American research universities. This model differed from prevailing practices in Europe and in other parts of the world: There, government funds were directed to federally sponsored agencies that would hire the researchers directly.

In the immediate postwar years, a large percentage of federal dollars went to a relatively small percentage of institutions. The hegemony of the East Coast Ivies and other private institutions was broken when competition sprang up from places like Stanford and the University of California's system of universities and the Big Ten schools.

There was also intense political pressure in Congress to distribute the funds more evenly around the country.

Another development in those years was the creation of federal research laboratories where university-based academics could participate in collective endeavors. When concerns began to arise about the preoccupation of research funding with science and engineering and defense-related projects, there emerged new entities such as the National Endowments for the Humanities and for the Arts, which made federal moneys available to faculties in the humanities, the fine and performing arts, and the social sciences.

One outcome of this fermentation was that the pecking order among American universities, and within the institutions as well, changed dramatically. New respect was given to institutions that could bring in substantial federal dollars and thereby attract research-based faculty. Soon all universities were under pressure to emulate this model and seek a share of the action.

A RESEARCH DILEMMA

At one point in his writings, Thomas Aquinas makes the claim that one cannot be a true metaphysician until some time in late middle age. That's because, for Thomas, metaphysics was the central subdiscipline of philosophy, and in order to have the capacity to understand metaphysical problems one needed long experience of life. This is akin to the truism that although one may be blessed with knowledge at a young age, wisdom requires extensive experience of life. This view conflicts with the mechanics of contemporary graduate education and research. American higher education today takes it for granted that there should be a time limit within which the Ph.D. is completed, followed by a finite span of time, normally six years, until teachers are evaluated for promotion to associate professor with tenure. That places an onus on young faculty to display sufficient ability and scholarly work in a few years' time to confidently predict a lifelong career of scholarship.

Yet it is the nature of scholarship to require years and often decades of research and reflection in order to yield results of the highest quality. Consider, for example, those scholars in the humanities who spend a whole career working on the papers of a single American president, or creating the definitive biography of some famous figure in political or cultural life. The Manhattan Project scientists and those involved in the early stages of space exploration would claim that their achievements were possible only through the efforts of hundreds of scholars whose work was hard to differentiate in terms of the contribution that they made.

To say that one can only be expected to produce mature work after the passage of time differs from observing that many academics change research focus in the course of a scholarly career, either as a result of changing interests or because of shifts in the availability of research funding. When the superconductor supercollider project was canceled by Washington a few years ago, many physicists were forced to find new areas of research endeavor. Other scholars suffer similar fates because of the vagaries in funding of the National Endowment for the Humanities and the National Endowment for the Arts, both of which have been under severe retrenchment pressures in Congress. When lawmakers mandate that 10 or 20 percent of the budgets of the National Science Foundation or the National Institutes of Health must be directed toward "practical" research projects, that priority-setting is felt in all American research universities.

TIME AND SPACE

Clearly, then, a central constraint related to graduate education and research is time. For one thing, this acknowledges that the individual researcher or group may take years or decades to produce a mature result, and in the interval it is often difficult to be certain that any fruitful results will emerge. For another, time limitations mean that the individual must constantly make priority choices among the multiple responsibilities of the professoriate to keep research, teaching, and service in balance. On top of that, most faculty engaged in research feel under constant pressure both to develop fundable research proposals and then to achieve their research goals within the supported span of time. This probably does not differentiate the American university from other high-pressure professional areas of endeavor, but it can lead occasionally to premature publication of results—or, in the worst case, to contrived results.

A second set of constraints has to do with space. Depending on the field of study and the methodologies and instruments employed, the space required for scholarly endeavor can vary considerably. The sophisticated instrumentation and computer support required for certain kinds of laboratory-based research in the sciences and engineering can add a considerable sum to the overall cost for a single project. That's why national laboratories have been so popular in physics and some of the other experimental sciences.

Space in this sense refers not merely to having room to move around in or adequate room to accommodate several participants in a research project, but also compatible space for multiple projects that might require the same research equipment. For many nonlaboratory disciplines, the issue of space has to do chiefly with access to research materials in libraries or over the Internet. From this perspective, space is a function of the capacity for intraconnection with materials such as relatively obscure journals. For instance, much research in the humanities, law, and business requires access to databases, and computer networking has increased exponentially the ability of the individual professor to be connected to these materials. For these individuals, the notion of dedicated space might be as basic as a comfortable room in a research library. In other disciplines, space can refer to research sites far distant from one's home campus: the anthropologist who travels to exotic locations or the archaeologist who oversees a dig in the middle of a desert needs sufficient time and support so that these spaces can lead to insightful research results.

University administrators often meet with skepticism the expressed need for new buildings and space renovations. The reason is that the modern research university has an endless demand for more space. Despite a relatively stable student body size over the last couple of decades, for example, Notre Dame has considerably expanded its academic facilities—partly because of rising standards for the quality of faculty offices and laboratories, and partly because of rising aspirations among faculty who are committed to research. The simple provision of computer access in faculty offices, as well as in departmental and college offices, has led to a new standard for how big one's private space, or a group's collective space, needs to be to promote the very best environment for research.

Another influence on the demand for space is the sheer quantity of information now available. Research universities tend to have multiple libraries, with convenient branches near college and departmental offices. As more publications result from increased research faculty, there is no end in sight to the demand for additional library space. None of this means that everything must be done that's possible to do. But there's no avoiding the fact that the space needs of the academy keep ratcheting up.

SCHOLARLY CAREERS

Looking at the scholarly contributions of the typical faculty member, one notices a resemblance to a bell curve—that is, early in his or her career the professor develops independence from graduate school mentors and establishes a distinctive scholarly direction; sometime in the middle to late-middle range of a career the greatest research results take place; after that, one produces less frequently and less distinctively. True enough, many faculty members maintain distinction over a whole scholarly career, but it is unusual to be equally productive from the beginning to the end of a career that might reach the seventies.

This pattern raises questions about whether the modern academy ought to reevaluate the way we think about the contributions individuals can make at various stages in their lives. Perhaps a better assignment for those in the latter part of a scholarly career would be to mentor younger faculty colleagues and graduate students, or to make a more focused contribution in administrative leadership, or to represent the department, college, or university in national and international organizations. I do not suggest writing people off or ending a career of scholarship prematurely; I merely propose that we think about such a career in a fresh way.

One of the persistent criticisms of the modern research university is that internal pressures related to promotion and prestige have generated too much unworthy or irrelevant scholarship. More than fifty-thousand books a year are published in the United States, and many times that number of journal articles. Unless a faculty member is willing to forgo sleep and any semblance of personal life, it is hard to imagine keeping up with all the relevant literature in one's own field, much less in broader areas of scholarship.

Perhaps this challenge has been simplified a little by computer databases, but it still seems clear that the academy is being overwhelmed by information accruing from research. On top of quantity, there's the matter of quality: If a researcher feels under pressure to produce results too quickly, it is unlikely that the resulting insights will be as finely tuned as they could be. Think, for example, of someone writing a biography of George Washington. The available resources might take a decade to absorb, and unless the work was begun in graduate school as part of a doctoral dissertation, it's highly unlikely that the biography would be publishable until some time after the decision for tenure would have to be made. One could display the early results as a kind of work in progress, of course, but that tends not to carry the same status as a finished product.

In the scientific disciplines, this problem is addressed in part by the tradition of the post-doctoral research appointment, which gives scientists a two- to five-year window to get a head start on research before taking on full-time teaching and research. The same purpose can be served in some areas of research and scholarship by government appointments or a period of work for a corporation. Under either of these circumstances, by the time an individual goes on the job market, he or she is apt to be more mature in scholarly activity and more productive of high-quality work. But in those disciplines where post-doctoral research opportunities are not available or not commonplace, young scholars must either establish a major surge of activity early in their careers or else to take on smaller, more manageable projects.

When I first became an administrator, one of the challenges I found in evaluating people up for promotion was the differing standards of what was considered high-quality publication. In some disciplines, one or two books are deemed necessary for tenure, especially if they were published by university publishing houses. In other areas of scholarship, articles in major refereed journals are the most prestigious way to claim one's place within the discipline. One reason for the proliferation of scholarly journals is the limited number of places available for both junior and senior faculty to get published. But when a group of scholars finds it hard to publish in the major journals, they have the option of starting one of their own. And if university publishing houses are not open to certain methodologies, aggressive directors may come along and make their mark by promoting new lines of scholarly endeavor.

The question in all this is, does it make any difference how wide the audience is for the results of scholarly research when they are published? Should it make a difference? If a book sells only a few copies to university libraries that buy on consignment, or if a cross-check of libraries finds that no one has ever checked out the work, should this disqualify it from being considered worthy? If an article in a scholarly journal is not referred to even once over the course of a decade, does that mean it will never make its mark?

One tendency we all have in the academy is to defend scholarship for its own sake. And it's true that any scholar will inevitably pursue blind alleys of work, but publishing about one's mistakes as well as one's successes can legitimately contribute to the overall search for the truth. And the unread book or article in one generation or century has in a few instances turned out to be the blockbuster in the next.

Still, these defenses of the life of inquiry do not necessarily mean that everything should be published. In every scholarly field there is a consensus that some percentage of publications are simply junk, unworthy of attention. I think we can say at a minimum that all fields of scholarship need to exercise more discipline. Editorial policies should be clear about what kinds of material is worthy of publication. To seek a voice is not necessarily to command an audience. To be convinced that one has something to say does not ensure a positive response.

One answer to this dilemma is to ask a person who's up for a promotion to present two, three, four, or five examples of his or her best work, so that judgments are made not so much on quantity as on quality. Colleagues may well be aware of the extent of one's publication record, but it is both liberating and healthy to be asked to present only one's best material at such pivotal times.

ACADEMIC PUBLISHING

University presses make a distinctive contribution to American intellectual life. Often they are the only places willing to publish manuscripts with a limited retail market. Small- to medium-size university presses tend to concentrate on areas of institutional strength and publish materials that are pertinent to the institution and its faculty. The University of Notre Dame Press, for example, focuses on such areas of our academic strength as Medieval literature, Irish studies, Latino studies, Catholic moral theology, and American Catholic history.

Most university presses, ours among them, not only have a director and an editorial staff but also a faculty committee that reviews manuscripts submitted for publication in order to ensure fairness in the editorial decisions.

Because the standards of these presses are usually quite high, their decisions to publish are taken seriously by tenure and promotion committees. As for commercial publishers, their number and diversity makes it much more difficult to be certain how they reach decisions to publish. In evaluating faculty whose books are published by commercial presses, the normal questions are the quality of the publishing house, the intended audience, and the impact the book might have on intellectual debate and discussion.

For university administrators and governing boards, the status and financial underpinnings of a university press are complicated indeed. In a few instances, endowments help subsidize the costs of production. In the case of older university presses that are quite large, the size of their annual lists and the respect they enjoy in intellectual circles assure a good bottom line. But at small and medium-size university presses, there is constant anxiety about survival and about the size and quality of the publication list. One recent trend in such houses is to try to find a best-seller or two to help subsidize the rest of the publication line. In some cases a single author may be the saving figure for the entire press. Some university presses have been disbanded when they became major financial losses for their institutions. Several others have survived by combining operations, particularly at the distribution level.

One goal of university presses is to make books available much longer than commercial houses typically do, but this, too, can be a financial strain. As an area of interest to benefactors, university presses have not proven especially attractive, perhaps because their story is not effectively told or perhaps because there are fewer natural constituencies for presses than for other units of the institution. I am convinced that properly run university presses are another way by which universities can make a major contribution to the quality of intellectual life of the culture. But I also believe we need to be more astute in the way we oversee these operations, and that that we must seek more effective formulas for solvency.

SCHOLARLY JOURNALS

Most universities produce a number of scholarly journals, usually edited by faculty members and sometimes involving students. The classic examples of student participation are law school journals. It is prestigious to be chosen as student members of the editorial board of such journals, and they therefore enjoy well-prepared and energetic student staff members who do much of the grunt work. Some university journals, in contrast, are entirely entrusted to the editorship of a single member of the faculty, with assistance from colleagues across the country or the world. Having the university's name on the mastheads of such journals is one way of making a mark among peer institutions, and often some university subsidy is provided. When faculty are being wooed from another institution, one of the inducements used to lure journal editors is to promise a higher level of subsidy.

Some university-based journals have long and distinguished histories; others come on the scene as new subfields develop in a discipline or new methodologies emerge. The kind of reception these new journals gain depends on their quality and the regard in which the editor or editors are held. The cost of publishing a few journals may not make a major dent in the academic budget, but if such journals proliferate, the impact can soon become significant.

The last thing a university wants is to have its name identified with second-rate or inferior publications. So it is important to conduct periodic evaluations of university presses and journals through some built-in institutional mechanism.

Institutes and Centers

An interesting facet of university life at the end of the twentieth century is the role institutes and centers play in the educational process. While there is no uniform agreement on how to define these terms, in most modern research universities institutes have more financial backing and a greater breadth of operation than do centers. Institutes are normally configurations of scholars, supported by funds generated from endowed, federal, or philanthropic sources, who undertake focused interdisciplinary research and scholarship. Centers have much the same look, perhaps with narrower objectives. Both institutes and centers are growing in importance as vehicles for interdisciplinary and intercollegiate engagement. As a result, many of the federal funding agencies have turned to these entities to maximize the impact of their financial support.

The most visible institutes and centers exist in dedicated space, often in a separate building. It is not unusual to walk around the neighborhoods surrounding long-established research universities and see signs on older houses proclaiming an institute or center. Depending on size and complexity, institutes and centers typically have a director and one or more full-time staff members, as well as a faculty advisory board and, often, an outside advisory board that serves as a means of attracting future benefaction and of soliciting advice from nonacademic professionals.

On many university campuses, institutes and centers are among the most prestigious academic units. They provide pass-through funding for interested faculty, hold seminars and conferences, publish journals and collected papers, and otherwise try to have an impact on the state of discussion of some problem or area of study. The great difference these entities have from departments, colleges, or schools is that they do not generate courses but are given over almost exclusively to the scholarly enterprise. The danger is that they may preempt the energy and attention of faculty to the detriment of other responsibilities within their academic units.

In most cases appointments to institutes and centers require the cooperation of a department and college, and this can lead to tension between the priorities of the institute or center and the department's needs for faculty to be in the classroom. It requires some degree of diplomacy and persuasiveness to ensure that this relationship remains smooth. Departmental faculty who do not directly benefit from the work or the financial support of the institutes and centers can easily become jealous of their colleagues' prerogatives, and see them as symbolizing a new and disadvantageous kind of academic pecking order.

At Notre Dame, our academic strength and visibility have benefitted from the existence of a number of prominent institutes and centers. Our Medieval Institute, Kellogg Institute (which focuses on Latin America), Kroc Institute for Peace Studies, and Ecumenical Institute at Tantur, Israel, are prime examples, as are the more recent Institute for Educational Initiatives, the Keough Institute for Irish Studies, and the Institute for Church Life, which promotes programs that serve the broader church community.

We have an even larger collection of centers: the Cushwa Center for the Study of American Catholicism, the Center for Applied Mathematics, the Center for Catalysis and Reaction Engineering, the Center for Civil and Human Rights, the Center for Continuing Formation in Ministry, the Center for Environmental Science and Technology, the Center on Ethics and Religious Values in Business, the Center for Pastoral Liturgy, the Center for Philosophy of Religion, the Center for Research in Banking, the John J. Reilly Center for Science Technology and Values, the Center for Social Concerns, the Center for the Study of Contemporary Society, and the Society of U.S.-Japanese Studies. Like those at most of our peer institutions, our centers come in a variety of sizes and degrees of complexity. Some have a long and distinguished history; others have been created as potential sources for future-focused funding.

Some academic activities of a concentrated sort, though perhaps not called institutes or centers, are quite similar to those entities. In our case, this includes the University of Notre Dame Environmental Research Center (commonly referred to as UNDERC) at Land O' Lakes, Wisconsin, and our Radiation Laboratory on campus. Schools heavily involved in government-sponsored scientific research might have several activities under the title of laboratory, but the issues are pretty similar to those of institutes and centers.

At their best, institutes, centers, and laboratories are effective mechanisms by which faculty from a variety of disciplines can gain sufficient funding to take on the big issues of the day. They are a useful way for a modern university to focus and magnify its research activity. Yet the bigger and more complex these entities get, the more they can develop a life of their own, resulting in a situation where the institute, center, or lab may stand in contradiction to the fundamental reasons for the university's existence. Because there's a danger that they'll become alien territory to anyone who takes seriously the obligations of teaching and service as well as scholarship, it is essential that university administrators and faculty pay close attention to the unfolding dynamics so they will recognize when a rupture is growing that could become definitive. While I am not involved myself with a medical school or a university-run hospital, I know anecdotally that this problem is especially acute in the relationship between universities and these high-cost, high-demand medical entities.

It has been our fundamental principle at Notre Dame that institutes and centers should be self-sustaining—able to live on the income from their endowments and/or the flow-through money from governmental, corporate, or philanthropic sources. There may be an occasional situation when an emergency or a major change in the environment requires a temporary infusion of funds to see these entities through a crisis. But if the difficult time is prolonged, it can only drain scarce resources from the other priorities of the institution.

Clearly, the selection of a director for an institute, center, or lab is a very important decision, because mistakes here can lead to inability to attract faculty participation or outside support. On rare occasions it may be necessary to close down such operations, either in the short term or for good. This is always a better option than allowing a second-rate, mediocre academic entity to detract from the academic quality of the institution.

At Notre Dame we have a wonderful center of art, the Snite Museum. The existence of this facility acknowledges the fact that museums offer yet another way by which the research and collecting activities of a university can be made available to the full university and the surrounding community. Galleries can be outstanding teaching tools, not only in arts classes but in other disciplines as well. It has been my experience that an important subsection of the broader community can become interested in the university primarily through this kind of attraction, and that a gallery can serve to broaden the circle of university interests and benefactions. Of course, art museums, like performing-arts centers, can be a financial drain if they are not properly directed and overseen, but at their best they can be an excellent way of broadening the environment for the fine and performing arts.

We have recently given a go-ahead for construction of a major new center for the performing arts on our campus. Music and theater, dance and film all should have an integral place in the educational life of a modern university. In some metropolitan areas these arts may be readily available in the community, but in a location like ours, even though there is a fairly well-established cultural tradition in our host city, we believe it desirable to contribute to the region's cultural life. Scholarship in the fine and performing arts is much different from that in other disciplines. For some faculty it involves performances with regular critiques, for others it means exploring the history and cultural underpinnings of aesthetic activity. It is also clear that all of the methodologies available in the contemporary humanistic disciplines are applicable to the world of the arts.

In the professional schools—in our case, architecture, law, business, and divinity—scholarly activities usually take a different form from those in doctoral programs. Much of the scholarship in professional schools is of an applied sort, although there is still a need for theoretical explorations applying a wide variety of methodologies. The field of ethics has become particularly important as practitioners of the professions find themselves overwhelmed by the social, cultural, and legal contexts within which they function. More and more professional schools are offering both courses and periodic seminars and conferences on professional ethics—an example of where the theoretical and practical can come together.

MULTIPLE WORLDS

It has been my experience that faculty who teach at all three levels—undergraduate, professional, and graduate—are more flexible in their teaching styles and more free-flowing in their scholarly interests. When I was teaching full-time in the theology department, I found that in a given week I might be teaching an introductory course to undergraduates and a preparation for professional-activity course to seminary candidates, while directing a dissertation for a doctoral student at the same time. Even though I would be touching on some of the same types of material in all these roles, the tack I took and the nature of the reflectiveness I was trying to elicit from students varied considerably. I enjoyed moving across these multiple worlds, and I highly recommend the ways that questions and responses from these different levels of students can change one's theoretical interests.

Ernest Boyer in *Scholarship Reconsidered*, a book that has received a large measure of attention from the scholarly community, laid out four areas of scholarship: that of discovery, of integration, of application, and of teaching. Discovery is the equivalent of the generation of new knowledge. Integration is the task of relating the new knowledge to the history of a discipline or the prevailing perspectives that attempt to unify disparate areas of research interest. Application is the effort to draw out the implications of new theories and perspectives for human engagement in the world and in society. Teaching is the stimulating and coherent transmission of this complicated process. I consider this a very helpful schematic to clarify the issues at stake. In the modern research university, the scholarship of discovery and integration are taken for granted as primary responsibilities. The scholarship of application and teaching are particularly applicable at the professional school and undergraduate levels. Ideally, the dedicated professional scholar will at various times engage in each of these modes of scholarship.

At Notre Dame we expect all four forms of scholarship, at least sometime in one's professional career. In my judgment, the quality of teaching (in the classic sense of the term) will always be enhanced if one is simultaneously engaged in the three other forms of scholarship.

In the end, I do not believe that research and scholarship are antithetical to effective teaching. Rather, they are the fount from which it flows. But it is crucial in the contemporary American university context that we not allow the research imperative (which has a momentum of its own) to so skew our priority setting and reward structure that we shortchange our students and fail to achieve the purposes for which we were established in the first place.

CHAPTER FIVE

Reading

When asked to describe what they expect of their under-graduate students upon the completion of their degrees, most higher educational institutions will invoke a common refrain—they should be literate, numerate, aesthetically sensitive, familiar with the promises and risks of science and technology, skilled in communication, analysis and problem-solving, open-minded, insightful, and generous in service and citizenship. Or put in another way, they should be well prepared to enter the workforce (or to continue their formal schooling) and capable of assuming responsibility for their own project of lifelong learning. In other words, a degree is not a sign that one is a finished product but rather an indication that the person is better prepared for all that life might offer.

For those of us faculty who operate in what is called "the humanities," a category in which both theology and literature are usually placed, there is no more fundamental academic and personal skill than the capacity to read texts (of whatever kind) with comprehension, sensitivity, and critical acumen. This may be the most portable and elastic of the abilities refined in the stages of one's formal education.

An inveterate and committed reader will be able to choose the scope of his or her areas of inquiry. The challenge will never be the boredom of one too many times through the tried and familiar but rather the human limitations of available time and sustaining energy. For some, reading in depth in a given field will prove more satisfying than an endless pursuit of unfinished endeavors. But the central point remains the same—reading provides access, it transcends the boundaries of history and culture, and it reaffirms the human desire to seek the truth, to savor beauty, to express the longings of our heart and spirit.

IN THE BEGINNING

Family constraints prevented my mother and father from going to college, yet I always considered them both to be bright and thoughtful people. One reason is that they prized education. Another is because they encouraged their children to read from the very earliest days. We always had newspapers, magazines, and books around the house. My mother in particular was a great storyteller and used to regale us at bedtime with tales that went on until we started to fall asleep.

I remember well the first book I read all the way through in one sitting: It was a *Hardy Boys* detective story, and reading it gave me a sense of both achievement and joy. I remember as well being enthralled by the Edgar Allan Poe short stories, poems, and mystery stories, and by a series of sports-related books by an author named John Tunis.

It was my parents' conviction that the important thing was not so much what we were reading at a given moment but that we got into the habit of reading with enjoyment. The presumption was that this would turn us into readers for life. And so it has turned out.

I sometimes suspect that the world is divided up into two classes: those who find words, phrases, and sentences intriguing, and those who are more fascinated by numbers. I have always been a words person. At St. Anthony's grade school there was a club where you could borrow books of interest to kids your age; you could take out as many as you wanted over a period of time. That was a great idea and one particularly suited to our school, where many of the students came from lower-middle- and middle-class families.

My grade school English teachers placed a lot of emphasis on vocabulary formation, spelling, and sentence structure. I enjoyed filling out the workbook exercises we were given as homework assignments: We would circle the part of speech, provide the right verbal ending, and indicate the adjectives and adverbs. We also did a lot of sentence diagramming, and I still remember the satisfaction I got from correctly diagramming a complex or a compound sentence. Today that style of education would be called basic, because it emphasized mastering such things as grammar and sentence structure. We took it for granted that the learning process involved building blocks, and that once we got the fundamentals down we would be ready to move on to more complicated and sophisticated materials.

In high school, when I took courses in Latin and Spanish, I became more interested in the etymology of words.

There is no doubt in my mind that a familiarity with Latin enhances one's working vocabulary: You learn how to pick words apart and see the function of prefixes and suffixes. The very act of translating from one language into another forces comprehension of the subtle ways in which words can be used in different language systems. The fact that Latin was the liturgical language of the Roman Catholic tradition at the time I was in high school meant that I was moving from the point where I simply recited prayers in Latin, particularly as an altar boy, to the point where I could begin to understand what they meant in the original language. This was both thrilling and demanding. And to undertake the same exercise in a living language like Spanish was to understand the ways in which different language systems functioned.

By the time I got to college I was a dedicated reader. No one had to coax me to open a new book or to broaden the range of my reading matter. I began to accumulate a personal library, primarily consisting of paperbacks, and I sometimes spent a fair percentage of my discretionary income on books. These acquisitions were things to enjoy, of course, but they also were a manifestation of my commitment to being an educated person. The fact that I switched my major in freshman year from chemical engineering to English meant that I was choosing an educational path in which reading figured heavily. It was a decision I've never regretted.

As an English major, I read not only the assigned material but often the secondary sources as well. If I enjoyed one work by an author, I was soon on the trail of other material by the same person. Like many students in the college years, my tastes expanded considerably. I read avant-garde literature as well as more traditional works. I read not only British, Irish, and American literature but also Russian, German, and other authors in translation. By the time I finished my bachelor of arts degree, I had read a lot for someone my age. I remember once starting to keep a list of all the books I had read, but then I figured it was an exercise in vanity and I discontinued the practice.

When my professional educational career shifted in the direction of theology and Christian ethics, I still kept up my reading in creative literature and eventually completed a master's degree in English along with the master's in theology that was my formal preparation for ordination into the priesthood. It was not until I became president of Notre Dame and looked for a teaching format amenable to my schedule and responsibilities that I was able to move back formally into the study of literature and film. Over the last decade I've taught a seminar course in which students read a cross section of materials, primarily fiction, from around the world. One of my goals is to get the students excited about reading, and to convince them that there is much to be learned about other cultures and ways of life through literature. I never use the same material twice in classes, and one reason is that it gives me a ready excuse for broadening my own horizons.

THE JOYS OF READING

I am not really sure what the pluses and minuses are when it comes to reading speed. Perhaps there are reading geniuses who can rush through material and absorb as much as the reader who plows along, but most of the educated people I know seem to read at approximately the same moderate speed. The important thing, of course, is not how fast one reads but the level of comprehension and enjoyment one gets from reading. As an administrator I am capable of speed-reading reports and relying on executive summaries to give me the gist of matters. It's pretty clear to me that skilled readers adapt their reading style to the material before them.

One of the more perplexing questions facing librarians and publishers is what the future may hold for books and other materials in paper format. Books, journals, and periodicals can be costly, and they take up space. Although computer technology has sometimes been interpreted as threatening the future of the book, recent studies at the national and international level have come to the conclusion that libraries need to be prepared to continue performing traditional tasks such as being a repository of books and periodicals as well as to take on the challenge of adapting to new formats for the delivery of information.

It may seem at first glance that it makes no difference how one reads material, whether off a computer screen or off a printed paper page, but I'm convinced there is a set of human factors that must be taken into account in this debate. The book as we know it, particularly in the cheaper paperback format, is portable, tangible, comfortable, and relatively easy to transport and store. Books can be purchased at one point in one's life and read months, years, even decades later. Books can be perused in automobiles, trains, and airplanes. As long as there is sufficient light, they can be read at any time of day or night. The appearance of a book's cover, its smell, and the tactile pleasure that accompanies turning the pages—all these infuse reading a book with qualities that appeal to our humanity.

For me, opening a new book triggers an unfailing sense of thrill and adventure, and a promise of encounter between the author and myself as the reader. To enter into the world of the creative artist is to be exposed to words, terminology, phraseology, and beauty that put demands upon us as readers. To sit back and wonder at a phrase well turned or a thought expressed with beauty and tenderness is to be touched at the very center of one's soul.

A friend once complained that he was only as smart as the latest book he read or the latest thinker he was exposed to. What he was saying was that he didn't possess an independent capacity for criticism. I mention this because anyone who reads widely has to be able to discern the difference between garbage and high-order achievement. There is always an aesthetic dimension that goes along with reading, particularly the reading of creative material. In the same way that some thinkers are more profound and all-encompassing than others, so some creative material is more beautiful, or touches the reader at deeper levels of human experience. To read widely is to enter into many different worlds, some of which are more attractive, interesting, and engaging than others. There is no substitute for experience in this regard. The eloquence of a Shakespeare, the romantic beauty of a Willa Cather, the transcultural insight of a Shusako-Endo, and the mastery of character development of a Flannery O'Connor are all standards by which we measure the achievement of other authors.

When I was a freshman in college I was advised that it would be useful, in order to keep mentally alert, to take a five- or ten-minute break each hour over a three- or four-hour study period. I have found this advice to be a sage and a useful technique when reading any kind of material. In my own reading I am accustomed to sticking at it for fifty or sixty minutes and then taking a five- or ten-minute break. I have also found that I like to read in six or seven different books simultaneously; that way I can move around amid a wide variety of types of material and keep a certain freshness. Some people complain that they lose their train of thought or find it wrenching when they try this, but I like the variety of styles, content, and even printed formats. I concede that it is difficult to begin a book, especially one that is complicated or dense in content or challenging in style, without covering a pretty good sampling in the initial session. Otherwise, you almost have to start all over again until you are properly immersed in the spirit of the text.

THE READING HABIT

Like all human activities, reading can be thought of as a type of habit. When parents of young children ask me what they can do to prepare their offspring eventually for college, I say, get them reading at an early age. What they read doesn't matter very much so long as they enjoy it. The fact that I spent some of my youth reading books that dealt with sports in a romanticized and dramatic fashion nurtured my interest in reading, even if it did not instill in me any profound wisdom or exposure to the nature of reality. A certain percentage of junior high and high school students seem to have an interest in reading science fiction or horror stories, and I don't think there is anything wrong with consuming the Stephen King corpus so long as they remain open to other types of material. Mystery stories can become addictive, but so can just about any kind of literature that provides entertainment and pleasure.

There has been sustained debate in recent years about the concept of the Great Books. When I was a junior at Notre Dame I took a two-semester course that covered the so-called Great Books, from the Greco-Roman period through the twentieth century. The selections were pretty traditional, and I will be eternally grateful that at least once in my life I was induced to read books that cover such a wide span of cultures and historical periods. To do this under the tutelage of a skilled professor was to be exposed to a world that I never would have known otherwise. Many of the so-called Great Books require close and attentive reading and are not for the faint of heart, while other material in this category has ceased to be stimulating in its own right with the passage of time. Nevertheless, I believe that there is a distinction to be drawn between works that are profound and stimulating and encompass a wide range of fundamental human experience, and other sorts of material that is superficial and undeserving of prolonged attention.

There is definitely a measure of relativity when it comes to judging what should be included under the rubric of Great Books. American authors such as Herman Melville, Nathaniel Hawthorne, Edgar Allan Poe, and Mark Twain have had shifting levels of support for being included. The decision is even trickier when it comes to appropriating the works of women and historical minority representatives. There is no doubt that many such authors were treated with a prejudicial standard at the time when they first composed their works. Now that we have a much more diverse population in our colleges and universities, it is important that some percentage of the material we cover reflect more directly the experience of people from multifarious cultural backgrounds. I believe that there have been great women writers and great writers from a variety of ethnic and cultural backgrounds, and if important works have been forgotten or neglected, then they need to be rediscovered. But it would be an injustice to all readers everywhere to exalt second-rate writers simply because they fit into categories of diversity.

The course I teach presently includes novels written by authors from just about every continent and many cultures. Chinua Achebe from Nigeria and Nadine Gordimer from South Africa can both be included as African authors. One is a black man and the other is a white woman, but together they capture a fuller sense of what it means to live and write within the African experience. William Faulkner and Eudora Welty both write as participants in the racial history of the South, but their work needs to be complemented by Ralph Ellison, Toni Morrison, and James Baldwin because the reality of race in America has implications far beyond the South. The growing body of literature written by Latinos, Asian-Americans, and Native Americans needs to be sifted by discerning readers, so that the next generation can be introduced to a literature of high quality that represents the richness of the American heritage.

It is really the task of a lifetime to read as widely as possible in the literature of not just the English-speaking countries but also of other cultures, places, and times. As I visit other parts of the world, I try to supplement and enhance what I've seen by reading broadly in the history, social analysis, and literature of each region and country and culture. Those who are not privileged to travel widely in a literal sense of the term can nonetheless take endless journeys through the vicarious power of literature.

There are more books published each week than any of us could read in a lifetime, of course. That can be viewed either as frustrating or as an opportunity always to anticipate the next book and the next adventure in self-education. I look forward to having a chance to read all the material I have gathered in my own fairly large library. One of the reasons why I enjoy wandering around good bookstores is that my desire is stimulated and my interests are peaked by that environment: I encounter books I didn't know existed, and I discover categories of material I suddenly wish to pursue. I experience the same sort of stimulation in a good library. Books and all the correlative forms of printed matter are a way in which the collective wisdom of the human species is made available across time.

CENSORSHIP

Because words and the ideas they convey have the power to change our perspective on reality and to motivate us toward certain types of action, they will always be potent tools in the hands of anyone motivated to use them to further some goal. Among the books available to us are those penned by pornographers and demagogues, mystics and romantics, revolutionaries and defenders of the status quo. There is no doubt that society has a responsibility to protect the young and the innocent from premature exposure to materials that can disenchant or corrupt, yet human experience suggests that those who move too quickly to censor books or journals are often motivated by reasons other than safeguarding the common good. A spirit of censorship can be employed just as easily to suppress religious holy books or printed constitutions as to prevent the propagation of methods to make nuclear weapons or poison public water supplies. For the adult reader, all things being equal, I believe that censorship is counterproductive. We need to help people learn how to make sound judgments about what they read and what is worthy of their time and attention.

In the Catholic tradition, the Index of Forbidden Books was a disaster, especially for those who take the life of the mind seriously. We need to be driven by a conviction that truth will out in the end, and that human creatures must discover the truth by a hard process of trial and error. The same objection applies to the politically motivated censorship of material that is considered antiestablishment or revolutionary. To be against censorship as a prevailing policy or practice, however, is not necessarily to disagree with efforts to control the accessibility of controversial materials. There should be legitimate efforts, both legal and otherwise, to protect the young, the immature, and those who would find certain kinds of material offensive or would not be able to handle them.

GOVERNMENT AND THE ARTS

There has been considerable debate in recent years about the appropriateness of using government money to support the creative and performing arts. The National Endowment for the Arts and the National Endowment for the Humanities are two agencies through which subsidies have been made available to artists in a variety of media, both on college and university campuses and elsewhere. There are also separate lines of funding for museums and libraries.

The main argument against such funding, aside from questions about the size of the federal debt and the burdens of taxation, is that it is simply inappropriate for the arts to be subsidized by any government. This point of view holds that private citizens and groups of citizens are the ones to decide whether or not to support the creative and performing artists in their midst. The market place, it is said, should dictate which creative activities will thrive and which will wither. Other critics, although not opposed to government subsidies in general, fret that the agencies distributing such funds are inclined in such liberal or avant-garde directions that they have lost the confidence of the American public.

There is no doubt that some excesses have occurred in the support of the arts. But when the evidence is examined, it seems that the vast majority of federal support has been directed at creative activity in local communities that simply would not be available otherwise. Comparable claims can be made for state financial commitment to councils for the humanities or the performing arts. Local public libraries, children's theater groups, ballet companies, and workshops for poets and playwrights elevate the quality of life of the communities in which they function, and they deserve support.

Federal and state subsidies have been crucial for the kinds of large-scale scholarly projects that cannot be completed even in a decade or two, such as putting together the collective papers of America's presidents or major authors and cultural figures. For these projects, not only is sophisticated training necessary but so is a long-term commitment of personnel and leadership. These activities often are organized and coordinated by university presses that lack the wherewithal to underwrite them from their own resources. A prime example of a successful commitment of federal funds for the common good is the existence of the Smithsonian Institution in its multiple locations. I personally have taken hundreds of tours on the grounds of the Smithsonian buildings, and it is always a delight to see the joy in the faces of children and adults alike when they come in contact with a well-organized version of their cultural history. The readers among us, as well as the viewers and the listeners, need to pay such attention to our cultural resources if we would not merely survive but flourish as a people.

THE INTRIGUE OF WORDS

One of the most valuable tools in the library of the dedicated reader is a good dictionary. For normal sorts of research on words and etymology, I like the tenth edition *Merriam-Webster's Collegiate Dictionary;* it is sufficiently contemporary that it includes relatively new words from popular culture, but it also has a nice mix of popular and obscure words from the past. The premier dictionary is obviously the *Oxford English Dictionary* in its multivolume form, but this is too complex and complicated for the non-scholar to use. Linguists tell us that many people function with a vocabulary of about one-thousand words and their derivatives—that's one reason why you can get into the language game of another culture by mastering a relatively small list of words and idioms. But although you may get by in life with a relatively small vocabulary, you will not be able to verbalize or perhaps even to experience nuance and subtlety and the creative expression of feelings and ideas without a much wider vocabulary. The dictionary is a symbol of the human capacity for precise and/or creative expression.

There are many ways by which an individual can enhance his or her working vocabulary. I always recommend to students that they buy one of those books that provide interesting and enjoyable chapters designed to enhance vocabulary through drills and other techniques. It is also helpful for an entering college student to keep a little log book in which unfamiliar words can be listed and defined and periodically reviewed. One student I know who chose this route was amazed at graduation time by the vast expansion of his vocabulary that had taken place over four years. A command of the language can be a source of satisfaction and pleasure. It can also enhance one's ability to get things done through effective written and oral communication.

There has been continual growth of specialized vocabularies in our time, often connected to particular areas of work or forms of communication. The most noteworthy example is the onset of what may be called computerese. We now speak comfortably about bits and bytes, interfaces, E-mail, and a whole variety of things that were unknown just a few years ago. Another specialized vocabulary is drawn from popular culture through the various styles of music and dance and videos. Anyone with a lively interest in popular culture will feel obliged to try to keep up with terminology from the medical profession, from television, from various hobbies, and from the wide range of ethnic groups that make up the American culture. The adept reader is one who has at his or her command a sufficient array of vocabulary to be comfortable both in highly sophisticated, formal communication and in pop culture and slang.

%$#@!+

Swear words are one form of vocabulary that can become habitual and contagious. Unfortunately, many people fall into the routine of spewing forth four-letter words in almost every sentence. After a while the shock value wears off and it simply becomes a sign of an uncultured or deliberately offensive individual.

There is something in the human psyche that desires an occasional way to express deep emotion such as anger or disappointment, so it is understandable why swearing and the use of Anglo-Saxon four-letter words, usually with reference to sexual organs or sexual activity, has been preserved, even in sophisticated circles. Because that is the way the world is and the way people interact, it is also understandable that in fiction, theater, and music there would be some employment of such terminology. For an adult audience, so long as the language suits the occasion and the type of characters presented, such words can have an honesty and integrity to them. It is still up to readers and viewers to decide whether they want to go on a particular journey with the author. What I find offensive is the intrusion of such vocabulary into otherwise common-denominator sorts of material designed for a popular audience, including children. There seems to be a formula, particularly in Hollywood, that requires every movie to have five to ten four-letter words as a manifestation of authenticity. You don't have to be a prude or an idealist to find this unacceptable.

11-ACROSS; 8-DOWN

In my family we had a Sunday tradition of completing the crossword puzzles in both the *Washington Post* and the *Washington Star.* I found this practice a great way to build vocabulary and also have fun, and to this day I'm an avid crossword puzzle solver. As my parents grew older and retired, they both enjoyed doing the crosswords so much that they bought two copies of the newspapers, so that each would have a chance to work on the puzzle independently. We always had a crossword-puzzle dictionary around our house to help us track down those utterly obscure terms that no one could remember.

Over the years, I have had periods of time when I quit doing crossword puzzles cold-turkey because I was too preoccupied with other responsibilities. But in the last five or ten years I have returned to crosswords for the pleasure of them. The present *New York Times* puzzles, in my judgment, are the most interesting and enjoyable to tackle on a regular basis. They are easiest on Mondays and most difficult on Saturdays. There are a lot of technical reasons why this is so: For example, the more obvious the head starts the puzzle maker provides, the easier it is to finish the puzzle rapidly. By the time you get to Saturday, there are fewer gimmes and much longer adjacent words to be completed. The Sunday crosswords in both the *Times* and other major newspapers are the most complex. Often there is a theme that appears frequently in the course of the puzzle. In recent years there has been the introduction of the use of symbols for words, and a kind of ladder connection that weaves its way through the puzzle itself. Usually there is no formal signal to the puzzle addict to be on the lookout for these complications, so it can bring great satisfaction when you discover how to break the logjam.

Anyone who works regularly on crosswords becomes intimately familiar with the quirks of the English language and the prevalence of various vowels and consonants in the construction of words. They also learn a selective vocabulary from other languages, along with the first and last names of some well-known individuals and others whose claim to fame is simply that their name contains multiple vowels. One way to guarantee children a high level of fame would be to give them names like Aardvark or Eero or Ono.

Doing crossword puzzles, especially the complicated and sophisticated kind, can turn into an addiction and a waste of time, of course. Yet I have found them to be a source of relaxation and enjoyment, especially in the midst of a busy life. Among the habits they reinforce is this one: When you don't know something, look it up. In the process you may learn something new. In this sense, learning can be fun for a lifetime.

COMPUTERS AND NEWSPAPERS

There is no doubt that the computer has enhanced readers' access to a wide range of information and data in very handy form. The Internet and the World Wide Web have brought the world closer together in a significant sense of that phrase. Even in their dorm rooms or homes, students and scholars can enjoy access to a sophisticated "virtual library." This is a great asset and should be cultivated both on and off campus.

Yet there are serious concerns about the computer screen as a user-friendly format for reading. A kind of depersonalization happens to the person who spends countless hours in front of a computer screen, for whatever purpose. The computer is a tool, just like the typewriter, the telephone, the radio, and the television set. It makes some things easier but it also complicates our lives. Having dictionaries and encyclopedias and other reference material on-line is a great advance for those with computer access, but such access involves expense, and this needs to be included in the calculus of benefits and deficits. I suspect that there will always be people like me who prefer the physical presence of basic reference material in my personal library.

In short, I do not believe that the computer will replace the book or even the magazine or journal. The two approaches to information storage and retrieval will exist simultaneously and serve different purposes, in the same way that television did not replace the radio but rather transformed the way that these media would be available. Just so, it's my opinion that the book will be with us far into the future.

Newspapers, magazines, and journals have always been an important part of my life. On a typical day I read four or five newspapers: usually the *New York Times*, the Chicago *Sun Times* and *Tribune*, the *South Bend Tribune*, and the *Observer*, the campus student newspaper. If I am traveling, I usually pick up *USA Today* and a local newspaper.

In my judgment the quality of most big-city newspapers has been declining, especially in coverage of national and international news. The number of informed columnists carried and the attention to both the positive and negative aspects of contemporary events has given way to an unfortunate preoccupation with tragedy, disaster, and scandal. Nevertheless, newspapers at their best still offer a convenient way of plugging in daily to the wider social and political context within which we live and function. They provide a different kind of access than radio or television. The several media should be seen as complementary and not involved in a zero-sum game for survival.

When you read any newspaper on a regular basis, you come to recognize its biases and prejudices, and you can take them into account in discerning the objectivity of a particular story, especially one that deals with a controversial issue such as abortion, economic policy, or the influence of religion on everyday life.

In addition to newspapers, I subscribe to a wide variety of magazines and journals. This includes everything from *National Geographic* and *Sports Illustrated* to *Commonweal* and *America* to *World Press Review* and the *Wilson Quarterly* to *Theological Study* and the *Journal of Religious Ethics* and *Chicago Studies*. As an educated person, I have a wide variety of interests. As a theologian and administrator, I feel the necessity of staying on top of certain specialized fields and the broader cultural horizon of the national and world community. I read *Fortune* and *The National Catholic Reporter.* I read the *Chronicle for Higher Education,* *Lingua Franca,* and a whole host of other magazines dealing with my areas of specialization as an administrator.

Magazines and journals are ways of keeping up, of being better informed, of testing one's own ideas against the prevailing opinions of the day. I can think of ten or twenty other magazines and journals that I'd find interesting if I had more time, but I have made my choices and am confident that the regular reading of the magazines and journals I've incorporated into my professional life allows me to be better informed and more effective in the roles that I play.

A dedicated reader is always only a step away from adventure, romance, enlightenment, or laughter. The next book may be the one that clarifies our confusion, inspires us to action, or puts us in touch with the living God. Through reading we interact with the human family in all of its variety, in its moments of peace and war, in its myths and stories, in its aspirations and failures.

May our days and nights of reading be filled with wonder and delight.

Part Three

The Collegiate World

CHAPTER SIX

Residentiality

Although a number of institutions of higher education in the United States, particularly community and junior colleges, provide no student residences, the residential-college model is a peculiarly American phenomenon. On-campus housing is rare in the rest of the world, with some notable exceptions such as England's Oxford and Cambridge universities, where the very heart of the institution is its residentially.

In this country, most liberal arts colleges have a residential tradition, as do many prestigious universities, especially those with one hundred years or more of history behind them. In our state university systems, on-campus housing is normally provided for first-year students and any upperclass students who care to utilize it, but many students move off campus as sophomores and never move back. Except for international students, graduate students at most institutions have to find their own housing, usually in the neighborhoods around the campus.

When Notre Dame was established, it was modeled

on a French boarding school, and through much of our early history the Main Building was the site of just about everything—classrooms, the dining hall, the chapel, and housing units—for students and for many of the faculty as well who were religious community members. As the student body grew, dormitories were constructed to maintain the on-campus living tradition. Today we have twenty-six dormitories for single students and a large complex for married students. About 85 percent of our undergraduate students and some 30 percent of our graduate and professional students live on campus.

From the beginning, Notre Dame was fairly severe in its expectations for personal regimen and discipline. There was little privacy, and rigorous rules governed student behavior. In this we were not dissimilar from many non-religious U.S. campuses. The big change came after World War II, when entering classes included many veterans of the European and Pacific theaters. It made no sense to ask these older and more experienced Notre Dame students to conform to the old rigid norms. From the 1940s until today, at least from the perspective of alumni from the earlier period, the university has continuously accommodated itself to the prevailing ethos of the broader culture.

Still, there is much that distinguishes the 1990s Notre Dame model of residentiality from those of our peer institutions. The first distinguishing mark is the presence in each dormitory of significant adults with responsibility: rectors and assistant rectors. The rectors, at least, live in the dorms twenty-four hours a day, 365 days a year. These people consider the residence hall their home, and they share with the students a common life and a high degree of availability.

Rectors play a multiplicity of roles during the course of an academic year, supervising the hall's operation, managing the physical plant, serving as counselors and disciplinarians, promoting community spirit, and, usually, functioning as pastors. Most of the rectors at Notre Dame over the years have been religious. The vast majority of the men have been priests and brothers of the Congregation of Holy Cross, while the women have come from a variety of religious communities. The assistant rectors are usually professional students in the law school, MBA, or master of divinity programs. There have been some lay rectors, but they recognize that among other responsibilities they are called to play a religious role in the life of their students.

The Notre Dame model places heavy demands upon rectors. They have to be good with names, interested in young people, flexible in their personal schedules, resilient when things go wrong, able to handle such crises as a death in the family or an academic failure, and generally able to stay focused on the essential things while being constantly sought out for help with lost room keys, stopped-up sinks, or getting the next-door neighbor to turn down the CD player.

Despite these challenges, the role of rector can be rewarding and gratifying. It allows one to enter into the lives of young adults at a critical time in their life's journey. It can lead to the formation of deep and lasting friendships. It can provide opportunities to encourage young people to use their God-given talents—intellectually, culturally, socially, and in terms of community service. The best rectors probably have the same personal skills as the best parents, with this difference: The rectors play an influential role in the lives of as many as one hundred to five hundred students at any given moment.

A second dimension of the Notre Dame model of residentiality is an expectation for the creation of community. The most common reference point at the beginning of each academic year in a dormitory is the notion of an extended family. Returning students are expected to treat incoming students with dignity and respect. There are no initiation rites, and everyone is considered roughly an equal. The word *community* comes up frequently in the rhetoric of both the hall staff and the hall student government, and it's defined as having respect for others as persons, including when there are differences. It also involves proper utilization of the common property of the dorm, and maintenance of a standard of common life that prevents anyone from being unnecessarily offensive. As in all families, these theoretical norms must be reinforced constantly in the ongoing life of the dorm.

A third dimension in the Notre Dame model is common worship. Because we are a Catholic institution, the chapel in each of our residence halls serves as a gathering place for community prayer. The Eucharist is celebrated on a regular basis, and other kinds of prayer settings are fostered as well. Just about every dormitory has its own musical group which includes both instruments and choir. The style of music and of worship is adapted to the needs and preferences of young people. Although no one is forced to attend services, and religious differences are respected, it is extremely gratifying to see the large number of students who worship in the dorms week in and week out. Our professional and graduate students have similar opportunities for worship with their peers, either in their academic or residential settings.

A fourth dimension comes under the rubric of *in loco parentis*. This notion of the university—or, in the case of the dorms, the rector and hall staff—standing in the place of students' parents may seem antiquated or oppressive to some, yet in its broad sense the phrase means simply that Notre Dame has a code of conduct to which it expects students to adhere. Our student guidebook, *Du Lac*, describes the norms of behavior the university expects of its student body. When these standards are violated in the dorm, it is the task of the rector and the hall staff to intervene and decide whether to handle the matter internally or forward it to the office of Student Affairs.

While it might seem, at this particular time in history, that the existence of a code of conduct would lead to full-scale revolt, the vast majority of Notre Dame students seem to live comfortably within these strictures. The number of serious disciplinary infractions is relatively small, although students complain a good deal about the rules and a few predictably find ways to beat the system even if risking their future status in the campus community.

The fifth and final component of the Notre Dame residential model is the traditions associated with the dorms, from the oldest (more than one hundred years) to the newest halls (just opened). Over time, every residence hall develops its own distinctive nickname, traditions, and special events. One mounts a humorous annual review. Another sponsors a campus-wide regatta. Another produces an annual talent show during one of the home football weekends. Another lets out a midnight scream each evening during final exams.

Much of the dorm spirit finds an outlet in interdorm athletic competitions, where teams have creative nicknames like the Vermin, the Wild Women, and the Screaming Otters. Some halls adopt their own service projects in town. These traditions, passed along from one generation to the next, are a source of hall identity. All new students, when they arrive, are welcomed into a rich and complex culture. And when new dorms open, the first set of residents has the privilege of establishing the culture.

CORESIDENTIALITY

A perennial student issue at Notre Dame is single-sex dorms versus coeducational dorms. In the short twenty-five years since the university began admitting women, the percentage of female undergraduates has grown to nearly half, and this transformation has taken place with a minimum of disruption and discontent. Nonetheless, our students push continuously for a more integrated coeducational environment. Almost all of our peer institutions, they point out, have coeducational dorms available on their campuses, and that includes Catholic universities and colleges. Because Notre Dame has resisted this trend, to some we seem an anomaly.

Why do we preserve the single-sex dorm? The first and most obvious answer is that this has been our tradition. It can also be argued that single-sex dorms provide a safe and comfortable environment in which men and women can be themselves without the pressure of undesired social interaction with members of the opposite sex. Particularly for women students, the same arguments that prevail in defense of single-sex colleges can be applied to single-sex dorms: Women have an opportunity to exercise all the roles of leadership in their own dorms, to cultivate a strong common life, and to focus on their academic responsibilities. When they choose to move out of this protected environment, they can do so on their own terms and on their own initiative.

To some extent, the same can be said about men in all-male dorms. They can play some of the roles, such as liturgical and social service leadership, that women might tend to dominate in a coeducational environment. They can unwind and be themselves without feeling they're in a spotlight or under the gun to perform successfully in coeducational dynamics.

Coeducation can take a variety of forms. In one model, men and women live in adjacent facilities and share common features like a dining hall or a study area or a chapel. More commonly, coeducational dorms have alternate floors in the same building for men and women. In more radical forms of coeducational living, men and women reside in adjacent rooms and share common bathrooms or shower facilities. These differences are pertinent to the debate, which at Notre Dame usually revolves around our prohibition of cohabitation and our system of parietal hours, which sets a time limit on when men or women can be in the other's rooms. As things stand now, visitation is allowed for much of the day, but at certain hours of the night the privilege ends.

The strongest argument for moving in the direction

of coresidential living is that it can contribute to the normalization of relationships between young men and women at an important developmental point in their lives. But as long as a campus community expects its residents to abide by prohibitions against cohabitation and maintains a parietal tradition, then the same counterarguments pertain.

At the theoretical level, I consider some forms of coresidential housing to be compatible with Notre Dame's expectations for behavior and conduct. Nevertheless, I am comfortable with our present arrangement of single-sex dormitories. This structure makes it easier to recruit rectors and assistant rectors in the Notre Dame tradition. It makes it easier to maintain a setting where sexual activity is assigned its proper level of significance. And despite student arguments about "normalizing" relationships across genders, I have seen no reliable evidence that our students or alumni are any more or any less socially skilled than students in, or graduates of, institutions with radically different housing arrangements.

Single-sex housing, to my way of thinking, has worked well for Notre Dame up to now and will continue to work for the foreseeable future.

ALCOHOL ON CAMPUS

Another issue of importance at Notre Dame involves the role alcohol plays in student lives—not that we are in any way unique in that regard. In recent years I have had the opportunity to chair two national studies that examined substance abuse among young Americans. The first study, conducted under the auspices of the Center for Alcohol and Substance Abuse connected to Columbia University, focused on college and university campuses. The data we collected verified what many of us knew from firsthand experience: Alcohol abuse is the number one behavioral problem on U.S. campuses, and the source of most campus disciplinary complaints.

The underlying causal factor in the destruction of campus property, the fuel in most instances of sexual and other forms of abuse, and the primary correlate in academic underperformance is the inordinate role that alcohol plays in the lives of some students. It surprises me that the faculties on our campuses have not risen up in protest over this problem. Maybe if enough evidence is accumulated, people will eventually sit up and take notice.

One of the surprising facts we documented is the growing amount of binge drinking by women in colleges and universities—the rate is almost the same as for men. Because women, on the average, metabolize alcohol more slowly than men, and therefore may become intoxicated more quickly, they are particularly vulnerable in the competitive social world of many of our campuses. We also discovered that fraternities and sororities play an inordinately negative role when it comes to the abuse of alcohol; the rate of binge drinking by fraternity and sorority members is off the charts.

Anyone with eyes to see who has regular exposure to the social patterns of our students recognizes that there's a problem. The question is, what can we do about it? Clearly, we need to take a more proactive role, and in some measure this requires educational programs. But education alone will not change behaviors; campuses also need

to provide well-structured programs of therapy and counseling. When our students recognize they have a problem, we must be equipped to respond to their need. But
even this falls short of our obligation because it comes
after the fact.

To really make inroads on the problem, most educators are convinced that student leaders must be motivated
to help change the peer culture. This quest goes against
the grain of the pervasive influence of advertising, where
the good life is so often equated with the consumption of
alcohol, particularly beer. Groups like Students Against
Drunk Driving (SADD) and religious groups that sponsor a healthier lifestyle can have an influence.

Students often complain that there's "nothing to do"
on campus, or insist that alcohol provides a way of relaxing on weekends. The pattern of binge drinking belies this
claim, however; it suggests that some students are drinking to excess every day of the week, or at least in the cycle
of Wednesday through Saturday.

The misuse of alcohol needs to be seen on its own terms.
Not only is it a causal factor in dangerous driving and
patterns of misbehavior, but it also has to do with our very
image of what happiness and human flourishing are all
about. I would argue that the reasons why drunkenness is
wrong and/or inappropriate are threefold: It reduces awareness, it affects negatively our capacity to make choices,
and it unleashes forces that reveal our dark side. The nau-
sea and vomiting that often accompany drunkenness are
reminders that our bodies revolt at such abuse. Sometimes
it takes a tragedy before our minds and spirits come to the
same recognition.

It is important to separate drinking alcoholic beverages from excessive use of and dependence on alcohol. One can advocate temperance without being a prohibitionist. It is also realistic to acknowledge that a majority of American families use alcohol in their homes on some occasions, so it is not surprising that young people see alcohol as a kind of rite of passage, especially when they find themselves on their own in a young-adult setting. Most young people come to college already experienced in both the use and abuse of alcohol. So we'll be going against the grain of the peer culture in hoping to establish a new standard and a new style of life.

Yet I have confidence that, over time, we can achieve a revolution in expectations. We have already done it where the use of tobacco and the need for exercise and dietary restraint are concerned. In many of the professional worlds that our students are preparing to enter, acceptance of alcohol abuse has already vanished. The three-cocktail lunch and the drunken Christmas party are, for many, things of the past.

Educators need to continue sharing ideas, programs, and initiatives from campus to campus. And as a society, we need to exam critically the influence that alcohol-related advertising has on the acculturation of our youth from grade school on.

OTHER DRUGS

Drugs other than alcohol are used on campuses, though they are not currently at the same level of concern as alcohol abuse. Most of us remember the sixties and seven-

ties, when the use of marijuana and other controlled substances was commonplace on many campuses. At the time,
this was equated with a loving and free lifestyle. In retrospect, most of us can acknowledge the harm that was
done to many in that period, and the false consciousness
that was part of the culture of that time. As a nation, we
are now overrun with drug use, which has brought ex-
treme violence to our cities, filled our jails, and left havoc
in its train.

It seems clear that the drug of choice among college
students today is alcohol. A growing percentage, however,
are experimenting with marijuana, cocaine, heroin, and
various chemically derived drugs. That which is forbidden always has a certain allure. That which promises instant gratification or heightened sexual pleasure is always
going to be attractive to some percentage of people who
can afford it.

One of the things that has changed dramatically in the
last quarter century is that today's drugs are so much more
potent. Marijuana is available now that's eight to ten times
more powerful than older varieties. Some strains of heroin
are so powerful that they can be used without needles.
Various forms of amphetamines ratchet up the potency of
agriculturally derived drugs by five to ten times. In other
words, even though the percentages of campus users of illegal substances seem down significantly from twenty or
thirty years ago, the risk to those who do indulge is
greater than ever. If nothing else, one can predict that
regular users of drugs will lack the discipline, focus, and
long-range planning skills necessary to thrive in an academic environment.

These substances are illegal nationally, and we must not allow our campuses or academic environments to be considered places immune from the prevailing standards of society.

Town and Gown

All colleges and universities have to deal with relationships between the campus and the surrounding neighborhoods. Campuses today employ large numbers of people, and for that reason are centers of stability for their communities. In spite of this, a certain amount of tension tends to exist everywhere between the campus community and the immediate neighborhoods. If there are large apartment developments and individual residences converted for student use in the vicinity, this tension is exacerbated.

Because a college has limited control over students who don't live on campus, misconduct in the neighborhoods can be hard to deal with, and incidents can quickly sour neighborhood attitudes toward the institution. These incidents may take a variety of forms, ranging from gatherings that turn into riots to more mundane irritants such as urinating on lawns, having large and raucous parties, and keeping the music on late and loud. Sometimes these problems can be mitigated by giving campus police some degree of hegemony over students living in the neighborhoods, but at best that's no more than a stopgap measure.

In my judgment, colleges and universities need to take the initiative in attending to the quality of off-campus living for their students, staff, and faculty. Being a good neighbor does not simply mean employing large numbers of people; it also means concentrating on matters that affect the quality of life of the entire community. Campus leaders can help by serving on community committees looking at matters of common concern. The university may also find it useful to sponsor special days on campus when the neighbors are invited to come and sample the resources of the institution. And of all the ways of moving the town-gown relationship in a positive direction, one of the most effective comes in the form of organized efforts of social service.

At Notre Dame, our Center for Social Concerns is an umbrella organization that oversees the activity of thirty-some student groups involved in service, either in the local community or across the country and even abroad. The range of community services is wide: tutoring youth, visiting the elderly, working with the retarded and the homeless, staffing neighborhood organizations, and living with paroled prisoners in halfway houses. The more that our students, faculty, and staff participate in such activities, the greater the chance that common ground will be struck, and that both the members of the community and the campus participants will see themselves as members of a common community framework.

Such voluntary activities can have real benefits in the classroom. Students who are active in social service often bring a different viewpoint and set of questions to their academic pursuits. Having been in touch with the raw side of life and having shared some of the suffering and pain that characterize the existence of too many members of our society, they will not be satisfied by stock answers to vexing questions.

For some colleges and universities, concern about the neighborhood has become a matter of sheer survival. The decline of areas around certain urban campuses has been known to dissuade prospective students and faculty from joining the community. Safety and security loom especially large in the consciousness of parents when it comes to choosing schools. Publicized incidents of robbery or rape or murder can devastate a campus community very quickly.

Whether it's a matter of survival or simply good neighborliness, our campuses need to be aware that the social worlds that surround them are more than mere backdrops to the activities of the institution.

Race on Campus

There is no more volatile area in contemporary higher education than race and ethnicity. This shouldn't be surprising, since it is our perennial national dilemma as well. Most of our campuses are much more inclusive and diverse than they were a decade or two ago, and the changes in the composition of both the student body and the campus workforce have brought to the fore a set of unresolved issues. In my years as president at Notre Dame, we have gone from about 7.5 percent to 15 percent in the enrollment of historical minorities in the undergraduate student body, and we've made comparable gains in the professional and graduate schools. Regrettably, we've been less successful in the recruitment and retention of minority faculty.

Along with the increase in numbers, we have tried to

be astute in the provision of support services. We now have a multicultural student office and a multiplicity of ethnic and racial subgroups and organizations serving our international students by continent and culture. In addition, we are doing a better job of celebrating ethnic and racial heritages in our common life.

Despite all this, challenges remain. The simple awareness that one is a member of a minority group in many social settings creates a level of alertness and sensitivity. Students in particular feel a heightened need to spend a certain amount of their time in the company of people who are like themselves or share comparable life experiences, and this can lead to accusations about the Balkanization of the campus, or a kind of voluntary neosegregation. The fact that there are few faculty members with a similar cultural background also makes it difficult for students to find role models and mentors who have instant credibility. On a religiously affiliated campus like ours, moreover, the fact that we are Catholic can be alienating to some who come from a different religious heritage. Finally, the role that campus security forces play and the reactions of fellow students can be seen as demeaning or challenging.

Our campuses must continue to strive to be inclusive and at the same time flexible in the ways they try to attain that goal. At Notre Dame, we have found that having branches of our alumni association reach out to African-American, Latino, and Asian-American graduates has been a real source of strength. Having special welcoming events for minority parents and students as part of freshman orientation has also been well received.

We must not allow occasional incidents of inappropriate behavior to stand in the way of our commitment to creating communities where all feel they belong and have a right to have their voices heard.

SEXUAL ORIENTATION

One of the more perplexing issues on college and university campuses today, especially among the student body, is the status and treatment of homosexual students. Matters of policy and legal protection have been debated frequently on both public and private campuses. At religiously affiliated schools, the discussion also includes theological and moral judgments that flow from the traditional teachings of the particular religious group.

At Notre Dame we have struggled to be both clear in our teaching and consistent in our practice. The Catholic Church distinguishes between homosexuality as an orientation and sexual activity between homosexual persons. The Church teaches that homosexual orientation is neither sinful nor evil in a person, but it also teaches that all people, regardless of sexual orientation, are called to live chaste lives in accordance with their vocation as single, married, priest, or religious.

Notre Dame has stated formally and publicly that we prize the gay and lesbian members of our community as children of God, entitled to the same respect as every other member of the community. We deplore harassment based on sexual orientation. We will continue our efforts to establish a more welcoming environment for all of our students, and to rid ourselves of unacceptable attitudes or behavior connected to sexual orientation. But at the same time, in the formal statements of the university and in its policies, we will strive to be faithful to the values of our religious heritage.

RESIDENTIALITY

Residentiality as a characteristic of many American colleges and universities refers to the effort to create a sense of community and collective responsibility in the extracurricular life of our campuses. In the place where students live, in the efforts and structures of the student affairs office, in the leadership provided by student government, in the whole range of student activities, each institution develops a distinctive sense of itself. As a result, students and families can feel a sense of welcome, can come to discover a sense of common purpose, can partake in a multigenerational sense of tradition, and can come to prize the new identity that they have assumed.

The more that particular institutions choose to be different from their peers in the ways that they organize the internal culture, and the more that the expectations and policies that prevail are out of synch with the broader American culture, the more imperative it is to articulate constantly the grounds upon which such choices have been made and such directions preserved. Single-sex colleges, historically black institutions, and those that deliberately maintain their religious heritage are particularly vulnerable in this regard. But I am more and more convinced that institutional distinctiveness, especially among private schools, is our greatest asset.

Nothing has served Notre Dame more characteristically and well than its strong residential tradition. It is the most obvious source of what some have called "the Notre Dame mystique." Coupled with our tradition of success in intercollegiate athletics and our pervasive religious environment, the concentration of on-campus living is at the heart of what makes Notre Dame special. Whatever changes in residential life occur in the future must always keep these fundamental values in the forefront of the discussion.

CHAPTER SEVEN

Intercollegiate Athletics

PERSONAL PARTICIPATION

Because I was relatively tall even in grade school, I played sports—baseball, softball, football, track and field, tennis, basketball, and a few games of our own devising—both in school and on teams sponsored by the District of Columbia recreation department. My neighborhood included a very large public recreation park called Turkey Thicket that had four full-size basketball courts, a football field, a baseball diamond, three softball diamonds, eight tennis courts, and a house for Ping-Pong and other indoor sports. I was the only sixth grader to make my grade school basketball team, and I was a starter in seventh and eighth grades. Although we won the city championships in both baseball and softball for the recreation department, I soon recognized that basketball was the sport that offered me the best odds of competing at the next level.

The next level was Archbishop Carroll High School—

the first integrated Catholic high school in the city and the pride and joy of Cardinal Patrick O'Boyle, then archbishop of Washington, who wanted Carroll to be an integration model for the city. I played freshman basketball, then made the varsity team as a sophomore. I had grown from 5'10½" in eighth grade to 6'3½" by the beginning of my sophomore year. Our team was reasonably successful that season, and the fact that we competed in the Baltimore/Washington Catholic League gave me a chance to travel for games. We ended up competing for the city championship against one of the public school teams, but lost in a close match.

In my junior year we launched what turned out to be a phenomenal school record of fifty-five straight wins over three seasons. That year we had four black starters and me. In senior year we had three blacks and two whites on the starting team and we competed in game circumstances against freshman teams from the Naval Academy, George Washington University, the University of Maryland, and Georgetown University—and beat them all. Our starting center, at 6'11", was John Thompson, who would go on to coach at Georgetown. One starting forward was Tom Hoover, who was 6'9" and 250 pounds and ended up playing seven years of professional basketball. The other forward was 6'4" Walt Skinner who would play for Catholic University. Our point guard at about 5'11" was George Leftwich, a future star at Villanova and the glue that kept our team together. I was the shooting guard.

Our team won consistently for a number of reasons: We played team-oriented basketball; we were almost impossible to guard because of our combination of height, shooting, and ball-handling skills; and we were fortunate enough to avoid serious injuries. We also had a reasonably good bench.

One of the specific dimensions of my experience in high school was that our team was adopted by the *Washington Post*, which, like Cardinal O'Boyle, saw us as a kind of model for an integrated city. Our success on the court, combined with our integrated starting team, resulted in many people embracing us who had no direct connection to the school. That fan interest has been kept alive by periodic feature updates by *Post* sportswriters.

The fact that John Thompson and I have fairly high-profile positions on the national scene is surely another reason why we have been covered in such depth over the years. Whenever I go back to Washington, I'm stopped by an interesting cross section of people, black and white, who recognize me from the old days. It may seem surprising that a large and complex cosmopolitan city should remember a high school basketball team so long and so positively. Yet one of the lessons I learned from those years is the depth of the personal investment many people make in teams. Successful teams can become symbols for issues and hopes and dreams well beyond themselves.

On to ND

During my senior year at Archbishop Carroll I was courted by more than fifty colleges offering basketball scholarships. That was an era when high-powered recruiting was just becoming commonplace. Of those fifty schools, one was very overt about offering illegal inducements, and a couple of others made ambiguous hints in that direction. Not only did I come from a successful high school program, but I also had excellent grades, so I was a reasonably good prospect.

I visited a number of schools and narrowed my choices down to Santa Clara, Notre Dame, and Villanova. I wanted to attend a Catholic university outside of my home area that had a college of engineering. I thought I wanted to be an engineer because my high school physics teacher, a priest, convinced me that anyone with ability in science or engineering in that post-Sputnik era had a moral obligation to help the country stay ahead of the Russians. But I wasn't cut out to be an engineer, as I soon learned the hard way.

At Notre Dame a number of things surprised me. The first was that there was no opportunity for formal competition in the freshman year. Although the freshmen practiced with the varsity team, there was no freshman league for them to compete in. This meant spending a whole year without facing intercollegiate competition, and I hated being stuck with no opportunity to show what I could do. The routine of practicing with the varsity every day took the same number of hours and was just as demanding physically, but with very few rewards.

The second thing I came to realize was that Notre Dame had second-rate athletic facilities in those days. We practiced and played our games in an old fieldhouse that served as a multiuse facility: In addition to basketball practices, it was the indoor track and field site, the place where the football team practiced on inclement days, the place where the wrestling and fencing teams practiced, and the site of the intracampus boxing competition known as the Bengal Bouts. The locker and training facilities in the fieldhouse were little better than the court itself, and the basketball facilities overall were not noticeably superior to what I'd had available in high school. The fieldhouse had one advantage, though: The students sat so close to the court they were an intimidating presence. Many teams, in fact, refused to play us after deafening experiences in the fieldhouse.

Today most major basketball programs have spacious facilities with excellent locker room and training accommodations. The spectators sit in comfortable seats, and some of the sport's income accrues from food, drink, and program sales. Once large facilities are built, however, it becomes more imperative to have a successful program to fill the seats. When I was playing at Notre Dame, almost all the spectators were students; today students are a minority of the crowd that comes to watch the Irish in the Joyce Athletic Center.

Still another difference between high school and college was the travel schedule. Notre Dame competed in every section of the country except the deep South, traveling by air to distant locations and by bus to closer ones. I learned from those travels about the challenges of keeping up with academic requirements and staying academically motivated far from the campus. Although I would faithfully take my books along on the trips, team camaraderie and my curiosity about each intriguing new place made it difficult to maintain the discipline necessary for opening them.

I also had to deal with disappointment and failure during my time at Notre Dame. Our most successful season was in my senior year, when we made it into the NCAA tournament but lost to Bowling Green in the first round. During my three years on the varsity we were a fair to middling team, yet our lack of success produced some complaining among the athletes. I think it fair to say that our coach was pretty well set in his ways and reluctant to adapt to the changes taking place in basketball. Every one of us was convinced that if we had gone to some other school, we would probably have achieved greater success.

OFF THE COURT

Although my years as a Notre Dame athlete were less than spectacular, at a certain point I was able to get a grip on my life and funnel some of my energies into nonathletic activities. I became a campus activist, involved in hall government, service organizations, and academic groups, and that was the best thing that could have happened to me. I clearly didn't have the physical talent to play professional basketball, and if I had, I would have missed the broader arena of extracurricular activities.

Without a significant scholarship, I could never have afforded to go to a school of the quality—or the cost—of Notre Dame. I had four years of college paid for—tuition, room, board, book money, and two summer sessions. All my family had to contribute was spending money and travel between Washington and South Bend. In return for its largesse, the university expected me to perform service in the dorm on a regular basis. The jobs we were assigned were not that difficult, and some gave us an excuse to get to know a broader cross section of the hall. This was surely true of mail delivery and night room check. Such chores seemed a small price to pay and were never a source of much grumbling among the student-athletes.

One thing that stands out in my memories of high school and college was that the athletes, by and large, had fun. For the participant, fun is what athletic endeavor is designed to be. Sports are stylized, ritualized ways of engaging in competitive endeavors, either individually or as a member of a team. They provide an opportunity to exercise and develop skills such as leadership, discipline, hard work, and resilience. They encourage setting goals and striving to achieve them. I have a special partiality for team sports because I've always enjoyed trying to mesh complementary skills toward a common goal. Basketball, for example, can be the ultimate ego trip if everybody goes one on one and tries to hog the show; contrariwise, it can be the ultimate team sport when people of different sizes and skill levels work together. To watch the Chicago Bulls in the Michael Jordan era, or before them the Los Angeles Lakers or the Boston Celtics or the New York Knicks, was to see highly successful teams where superstars and role players brought out the best in each other.

The various forms of athletic competition continue to evolve as rules change and equipment improves and the arena of play is altered, usually for the better. It is arbitrary that the basketball rim is ten feet high, or that the football field is one hundred yards long, but once those standards have been established, then the whole game needs to take them into account. The role of referees, umpires, or judges is to ensure that participants play by the rules, to assign penalties fairly, and to attempt to see that the final results reflect the nature of the particular encounter. No two games are alike, even if the same two teams are competing. There is an ebb and flow, a give and take, to every athletic contest. This is part of the beauty and the interest of sport.

THE GROWTH OF SPORTS CULTURE

The pivotal time for intercollegiate athletics in this country was the 1930s. As Murray Sperber demonstrated effectively in his book *Shake Down the Thunder,* the newspaper industry in those years was desirous of increasing circulation, and an effective tool to that end was the deliberate creation of a whole series of American sporting heroes and heroines such as Jack Dempsey and Gene Tunney and Joe Louis in boxing, and Babe Ruth in baseball. Perhaps the chief beneficiaries of this icon building were colleges and universities with major intercollegiate football programs, and none was more successful than Knute Rockne and the Fighting Irish. College football went from being a local and regional phenomenon to one that included significant intersectional rivalries: Notre Dame versus South California, for example, and Notre Dame versus Navy. The country was hungry for something to cheer about, and in the ethnic urban ghettos, where a high percentage of Catholics lived, it was exciting to cheer for a team that represented upward mobility and achievement. At Notre Dame, the Fighting Irish nickname allowed the team to be embraced by Irish-Americans who had a religious and cultural affiliation with a place many of them had never seen. What was begun by the newspapers soon spread to radio and television.

Today the media—as a quick check of any newspaper or the daily offerings on cable television will show—mirror the central place held by amateur and professional athletics in American life. Just check the number of pages a typical student newspaper devotes to athletics as compared to other modes of extracurricular activity, or observe the copious coverage of collegiate sports by national publications such as *Sports Illustrated* and the *Sporting News*. Whole networks such as ESPN and Sportschannel are devoted, twenty-four hours a day, 365 days of the year, to presenting live or taped sporting events. Talk radio also includes a fair number of sports-oriented programs.

There appears to be an insatiable demand by the public for coverage of athletic competition, as well as for programming that focuses on behind-the-scenes interviews with participants, coaches, and sports pundits. Notre Dame's athletic successes alone have spawned two weekly newspapers, neither connected to the university, that devote themselves exclusively to our teams, primarily football. It is possible for fans to learn the hobbies and preferred toothpaste of incoming athletes before they spend so much as a day on campus. Some individuals even make a living by evaluating high school athletes and keeping on top of the recruiting process, then publishing their evaluations.

One of the lessons my early athletic exposure taught me was the importance of learning how to deal with publicity and public relations. Because student-athletes in highly visible programs do attract media attention, we consider it our responsibility at Notre Dame to help prepare our athletes for these encounters. Like most of our peer institutions, we provide formal instruction in speaking technique, dress and appearance, and ways to prepare for the different circumstances the athletes might encounter. One perennial bit of advice we give is this: Always praise your opponents and teammates, in victory or defeat. While some student-athletes are resistant to even the best instruction, I think media training has served our student-athletes well.

It does no good to lament the distortion of priorities that all this reflects. As with any human activity, so long as there is a market there will be individuals and groups happy to provide a product. Media exposure, of course, can be used to tell a positive or a negative story about the institution. Most colleges, like Notre Dame, have sports information offices to provide material for the media and to respond to particular opportunities and controversies as they come along. Usually it is the responsibility of the athletic director, and in our case the executive vice president, to represent the university to the media in athletic matters. Insofar as we can, we try to provide an accurate picture and interesting copy. Only in those situations where personal reputations are at stake and the matter is inherently confidential do we refuse to furnish information. As a general principle, I think it is desirable for colleges and universities to be as straightforward and cooperative with the media as possible. If the results are sometimes disappointing, that does not distinguish universities from many other complicated public institutions.

A second byproduct of media attention to intercollegiate athletics is the opportunity it can provide for sources of income to help carry the cost of certain programs. The NCAA television contract related to the NCAA basketball tournament pays for the entire cost of the national NCAA office and also makes significant sums available to member institutions. In recent years, moreover, individual schools or conferences have been making independent arrangements for television coverage of their football games, and this can also be the source of significant revenue.

A more complicated and fluid situation exists with the collegiate football bowl picture. Participation in major bowl games is another source of significant revenue. But even participation in so-called minor bowls can be a break-even situation and provide a sign of year-end success and an opportunity to spend the holidays with alumni and supporters.

I am not prescient enough to predict what the future holds with regard to intercollegiate athletics on television. Some think that pay-per-view is the wave of the future; others strongly advocate national championship playoffs for football. Some predict that certain women's sports will grow in popularity through television exposure, thereby creating new sources of revenue to help cover the costs of the overall intercollegiate offerings.

Financing Athletics

When Notre Dame entered its contract with the NBC network to cover Irish home football games, it was done after considerable internal deliberation. There was growing evidence that the Collegiate Football Association arrangements were going to become counterproductive for us. Because we have a national constituency and were enjoying success on the gridiron, we were unique in our attractiveness to a national network. Yet our primary reason for agreeing to the contract was that it would provide significant additional funding, not for our intercollegiate athletic programs but for financial aid for all our students.

And so it has turned out. In the years since the NBC contract went into force, we have been able to channel tens of millions of dollars into our endowment for academic scholarships, primarily for undergraduate students. These funds are supplemented by income from bowl participation and from marketing our institutional logo—income that's likewise directed into financial academic aid. Although the NBC contract attracted some controversy at the beginning, I am convinced it was a proper step for us to take.

We are fortunate at Notre Dame to be able to underwrite both a large, multifaceted intercollegiate athletic program and a significant intramural program from the revenue generated by athletics. Many colleges and universities are not so fortunate; for them, the cost of running the intercollegiate program, at whatever scale, must come at least partially out of the operating budget. I do not see anything incompatible about this, since I think there is a good case to be made for the importance of offering intercollegiate athletic opportunities to the student body. But it does put greater pressure on institutional leadership to balance athletics spending with other programs.

For private institutions offering a wide spectrum of intercollegiate sports, the biggest expense is scholarships: Tuition, room, board, and related costs add up to a total that can be quite daunting. Other major costs incurred by athletic programs are coaches' salaries, travel, equipment, and the support of such personnel as trainers, physicians, and managers. There is obviously a wide discrepancy between transporting a small cross-country team in vans one hundred miles away and flying a complete football team and its support personnel from coast to coast or, on occasion, overseas. The number of coaches, the quality of the teams' gear, and the institutional standards for things such as weight training tend to be generated by the competitive environment at the different levels of NCAA competition. In some ways the demands are endless, and the arguments for what's necessary for a successful program are all plausible. It is up to the athletic administration, in consultation with the central administration, to keep a rein on expenditures for these programs.

Some aspects of the cost of sports can be tricky to analyze. Student athletes on full scholarship are a regular part of the student body and are therefore, in one sense, a source of revenue for the operating budget, particularly if their scholarships come from athletic revenues. The facilities used by intercollegiate teams for both practices and games are normally available to the broader student body, faculty, and staff as well, and in that sense can be considered a university-wide asset. Some schools budget the upkeep of their athletic facilities within the general university physical maintenance budget; others include these items specifically under the athletic department budget. How one does it makes a big difference when it comes to determining the overall cost to the institution of various forms of athletics.

Perhaps the most controversial cost in major athletic programs is the salary scale of head coaches, particularly the ones who coach the popular sports. Quite a few coaches supplement their university income with revenue from television shows, speaking engagements, and contracts from athletic equipment companies, and critics have made much of the gulf between coaches' overall income and the financial situation of student-athletes. What I think the future will bring in this regard is a greater formalization of the relationship between athletic equipment companies and educational institutions, so that money earned by coaches will be more controlled and equitable, and the institution will get its fair share of this income.

In a free-enterprise system, it is hard to argue that the outside earning potential of coaches should be unduly restricted, but we should at the least apply the same standards to coaches that we do to faculty—that they spend the vast majority of their time on tasks that serve the internal purposes of the university, and only a minority of time on outside activities.

As for paying student-athletes, I am opposed to subsidizing them at a level beyond that which is available to the student body in general. If they qualify for any support beyond their athletic scholarships, that decision should go through the same process used by the rest of the student body. I do not think student-athletes should be considered professional-athletes-in-formation. Any benefit provided to one group of student-athletes, male or female, in any sport, should be available to all student-athletes.

The greatest benefit we have to offer them is a relatively free education of high quality. This is what they'll need to sustain them through the rest of what we hope will be a productive, meaningful life. If the lure of immediate reward is too strong for them to resist, then they should be encouraged to join the professional ranks and leave their scholarships behind. If they wish to continue their education later on, they will presumably have the funds to do it.

TITLE IX

The Title IX debate—sparked by federal regulations requiring colleges and universities to expand opportunities for women in intercollegiate athletics, and to do it quickly—has at times been acrimonious. That's because while the will has generally been there, the means sometimes have not.

There is wide consensus in the academy that women and men deserve to be treated fairly when it comes to playing intercollegiate games. Where disagreement exists is over ways of achieving this goal, within available resource constraints and in a set span of time, without either eliminating some opportunities for men or finding additional sources of revenue to supplement women's offerings. At Notre Dame, where we recently marked our twenty-fifth anniversary of coeducation, we've had to make some fairly dramatic changes in the last couple of decades. With an undergraduate student body now approaching half female, we have added new sports for women and significantly multiplied the number of scholarships available to female athletes. We've also tried to upgrade the schedules and resources available to women athletes and coaches. I see the same effort being made at most institutions I'm familiar with.

The chief complication on many campuses has been the fact that the primary source of athletic revenues is intercollegiate football, which is also the largest program with male participants, and the costliest to run. I am not a lawyer, so I don't claim to offer a definitive interpretation of the legal realities, but I believe all of us are puzzled about how to count football in the context of Title IX regulations. It seems counterproductive to eat into the quality of a football program simply to conform to some magic formula that outsiders have imposed. A healthy and successful football program, after all, allows many institutions to channel substantial resources to all their student-athletes, male and female alike.

I would prefer to see a more flexible formula regarding women's sports than the federally mandated one. For example, if football could be counted as X—where X is eighty-five (the NCAA maximum for football scholarships) minus a reasonable number—then one could compute the number of scholarships for male athletes as X plus the actual number for all the other men's sports. If that number became the one used to compare with scholarship figures for women, I believe the result would be a fair distribution of resources.

The formula should also be considered in the light of two other considerations: first, the relative percentages of males and females in the undergraduate student body; and second, the professed levels of interest and participation in intercollegiate sports by male and female students. If, over time, the interest levels of both male and female students proved to be the same, then obviously the opportunities for intercollegiate participation should be approximately the same for both. But if, as some suggest, there are different levels of interest and participation for men and for women, then it seems reasonable to me to take that into account as resources are allocated.

Nor are scholarships the only pertinent issue in this debate. Even more sensitive, perhaps because they're so symbolic, are matters such as scheduling and the quality of locker rooms, uniforms, and equipment, where lack of parity can be glaring. Likewise, the sometimes elevated salaries paid to male coaches, especially in football and basketball, often rankle women who coach in comparable sports, even when the women's salaries are in line with general university standards. This disparity would change, of course, if some women's intercollegiate sports become more popular with the media, the public, and the athletic-equipment companies. The success of women's competition in the 1996 Atlanta Olympics suggests that significant changes in the attention given to women's athletics at both the amateur and professional levels may not be far off.

STUDENT-ATHLETES

One difficult area for universities with both high admission standards and division 1-A competition is the academic preparation of student-athletes, especially in our urban school districts. It is a national scandal that so many inner-city schools are centers not of scholastic excellence but of underperformance. In too many cases, the principals are not in control, the teachers are not well prepared, the physical environments are dilapidated, and the social circumstances are insecure and even frightening. Dropout rates in such schools are high, and few of the students have any expectation of enrolling in one of the country's premier institutions of higher education—except for those elite student-athletes who are recruited by the best colleges.

When lower-achieving applicants do gain admission, they find themselves in fairly rarefied academic environments, surrounded by highly qualified peers. This can be a source of consternation to student-athletes, especially on campuses where they are recognizable by their dress or appearance. Student-athletes often spend large amounts of time in each other's company, and this can reinforce a sense that they as athletes are unlike the rest of the student body.

Part of the answer to these problems involves academic advising for student-athletes. When a college or university admits any student, it is implicitly promising to do everything it can to insure that student's success. This is especially true in the case of student-athletes because of the multiple demands sports place on their time and attention. At Notre Dame we have developed an office of academic advising for student-athletes that reports directly to the executive vice president and supplements the services we make available to first-year students in general. Our system provides a regular counseling structure, tutoring opportunities, and ongoing assessment of the student-athlete's classroom progress. This personalizes the process but keeps it one step removed from the coaches, leaving them free to concentrate on the playing field or area.

In the end, of course, the student-athlete must do the academic work himself or herself. But we take pride in the success rate of our student-athletes in a highly competitive academic environment, and much of that success is attributable to the dedication of our academic services office. Here at Notre Dame, we operate by rules more rigorous than the NCAA requires. We expect our student-athletes to stay on track toward completion of a degree within four years. That means that the courses they take each semester and the grades they receive must indicate they're making appropriate progress. If their grades slip below an acceptable level, then they are declared ineligible to participate in their sport the following semester.

One reason we do not have a red-shirting policy for first-year student-athletes is because this practice takes away some of the incentive for completing a degree in four years. Students who do not participate in their sport during a given season, however, are eligible to apply for an additional year after they have completed their four years of academic eligibility. While this constitutes a kind of red-shirt possibility, it is strictly at the initiative of the individual student-athlete and requires approval of our board on athletics. It is not a matter left to the discretion of coaches.

One of the ways by which we facilitate the academic progress of our student-athletes is to offer them the option of attending summer school classes on campus. Thanks to this option, some carry a reduced academic load during their seasons of competition, while others use summer classes to accelerate their studies. Participation in summer school is never mandatory—it is simply one more method by which we try to help our student-athletes strike a proper balance between their academic opportunities and their participation in sport.

COACHES

It is worth emphasizing here that coaches share in the teaching mission of an institution. By force of words and example, they can help young people grow and develop their God-given skills. Coaches ought to view themselves first and foremost as teachers, and like all teachers they should live by the highest professional standards. As a former student-athlete myself, I realize that the dynamics between a coach and a team are different from those that prevail in the classroom between teacher and students. Coaches deal more explicitly with emotions, and with the need for constant motivation. They also deal with the physical condition of their student-athletes. While "playing hurt" will always be in the background as an expectation, the definitive judgment about the availability of a given student-athlete must be in the hands of the medical personnel, not the coach.

In the recruitment effort particularly, the coach should adhere to the highest standards and provide the prospect with a fair and honest assessment of the chances that he or she might compete effectively at the school's level of competition. The problem is, the rhetoric of recruitment has become so inflated that no one really takes seriously the import of the words used. The integrity of the coach and of the institution demands that there be a sufficient degree of sincerity and truthfulness in the recruiting effort. By the same token, institutions should treat their coaches professionally. Although coaches should not have tenure, they should receive evaluations on a regular basis. The win-loss record counts, obviously, but it should not be the only factor in judging a coach's performance. Coaching is a high-profile profession with many rewards, but there also are prices to be paid. In my experience, institutions have been much more consistent in honoring their contracts with coaches than vice versa.

Another challenge facing athletics in higher education concerns the employment of minority coaches and support personnel. Intercollegiate basketball probably has achieved the best record in this regard, far better, certainly, than intercollegiate football. But because the factors that go into the hiring of coaches are difficult to pin down, it seems to me that institutions need to approach the challenge in terms of affirmative action goals rather than quotas. When the opportunity exists to employ a minority coach or hire minorities for the athletic administrative jobs, that moment should be seized insofar as possible. In addition, NCAA institutions should collectively be running internship programs and other preparatory opportunities for minorities and women in order to meet the goals of future diversity.

ATHLETES AND DRUGS

In recent years, the question of mandatory drug testing for student-athletes has moved to the forefront of college athletics issues. One of the apparent anomalies of contemporary higher education is the fact that student-athletes face unannounced random drug testing if they participate in NCAA tournaments or other major competition, yet the rest of the student body is not exposed to such testing unless it is prompted by disciplinary procedures.

I am convinced that testing student-athletes for drugs has served, and continues to serve, an admirable purpose. It is intended to level the playing field by eliminating any incentive to use drugs either recreationally or as a means to enhance performance. Drug testing is capable of detecting all the major drugs, from steroids to marijuana to cocaine to heroin. There is some suspicion that certain forms of chemically based drugs may beat the testing system at any given moment, but whether this is actually so is unclear. It's a possibility that needs to be continually monitored.

Quite apart from the NCAA, Notre Dame a number of years ago began testing its student-athletes across all sports. We now use hair samples, which are less invasive but more comprehensive than the previous urine sample. We did so because there was growing evidence that some of our student-athletes were abusing drugs, and we wanted to send a strong message that we would not tolerate drug use. When student-athletes arrive at Notre Dame, they have the drug testing policy explained to them very clearly. The first offense leads to suspension for a period of time. The second prevents the offender from ever again competing as a Notre Dame athlete. The tests are administered by university physicians, and any positive result is communicated to the appropriate university authorities. Coaches are informed only after the fact, and they have no say in what the penalty will be.

I think this policy is a good idea for the simple fact that the temptation to use drugs for performance enhancement is quite substantial among student-athletes. This is true not only for steroids and other pills, but also for marijuana and cocaine, since many student-athletes believe that those drugs will inspire them to higher levels of consciousness and motivation. These drugs are illegal for good reasons, and that goes for student-athletes as well as for everyone else. I am unpersuaded that unannounced random drug testing is an infringement on the rights of student-athletes; on the contrary, it creates a much fairer situation for everyone involved in athletics.

ATHLETIC ADMINISTRATORS

The responsibilities of athletic administrators are anything but trivial. They propose and manage a budget; they supervise a complex set of operations involving coaches, medical personnel, trainers, student managers, student-athletes, and support staff; and they are often spokespersons for their institutions in the arena of intercollegiate athletics. It is crucial, then, that they wholeheartedly embrace the institution's purposes, goals, and standards. They must never let athletics be seen as something set apart from the rest of the college or university.

One of the most important skills for athletic administrators to possess is the capacity to handle the finances of their operation. Many athletic programs operate on a deficit budget when income from athletic sources alone is considered, and those who administer these programs need to make a realistic and persuasive case to the central administration for supplemental funds from the school's operating budget. Like all higher education administrators, those in athletics must strive to run an efficient and effective operation. They should be alert to containing costs as well as enhancing revenue. And when they do propose new sources of revenue, these must be compatible with the nature of institution. At Notre Dame we have found it useful to have a committee of athletic and non-athletic administrators examine all proposals for revenue enhancement to ensure that they have an institutional fit.

Athletic administrators must also see to it that all coaching personnel perform responsibly and consistently. They must not expect the impossible when it comes to win-loss records if the appropriate resources have not been made available. Evaluations of coaching performance should take into account multiple years of activity rather than focus on one year in isolation. But there are certain forms of misconduct that, once discovered, must be dealt with forcefully and decisively.

It is also the responsibility of athletic administrators to ensure that student-athletes are treated fairly by their coaches. It's important for these administrators to keep an open-door policy and to solicit actively the opinions of student-athletes about matters that affect their lives. At Notre Dame we have found it helpful for athletic administrators to interview graduating students to try to ascertain whether things have gone well or poorly.

Because athletic administrators are the prime university contacts with the National Collegiate Athletic Association, they should stay on top of proposed legislation and changing policy and procedures. They also need to be certain their institutions abide by the rules. This is most urgent when it comes to the recruiting process: Violations, even minor ones, should be reported quickly to the NCAA with an explanation of what's been discovered so a full investigation can be undertaken. There is nothing worse than trying to hide incidents, since that establishes a negative dynamic that can come back to haunt the institution. If an administrator or coach happens to disagree with the some of the NCAA rules, the only proper response is to seek a change in policy at the national level.

Institutions usually involve faculty in overseeing their intercollegiate programs in some fashion. Often these committees are a mix of administrators, faculty, and staff—they may have some student representation as well—and they provide a forum to consider and ratify internal policy decisions. They can also serve as a good place to air grievances or general concerns. The more the faculty as a whole is convinced that intercollegiate programs are being administered by the highest standards, the better it is for the institution.

On some campuses there are entities with a long and semi-independent existence known as "booster clubs." These groups are often involved in raising money for the support of the intercollegiate athletic programs. In the past, some of these groups have had an inordinately decisive role in setting policy for their institutions' programs. Recent reforms at the NCAA level have significantly reduced the influence of booster clubs, and I applaud the change. It is crucial that all funds connected to the intercollegiate athletic programs be under the direct supervision of the athletic administrators and, through them, under the supervision of the president or chancellor.

The role of alumni with regard to intercollegiate athletics can be controversial. Often an institution's fans include more than alumni—at Notre Dame we have our subway alumni, fans who have not gone to Notre Dame but have developed a high degree of identification with us. Some of these fans are "fanatics" in the pejorative sense of the term, with a distorted sense of the priorities of the institution. They allow the success or failure of athletic teams to be the source of their institutional loyalty. Almost all studies, including some we've conducted, show no direct correlation between the success of athletic teams and the overall health and well-being of the institution, and that goes for success in fund-raising and student recruiting.

Occasions may arise when athletic administrators need help from the central administration in curtailing inappropriate lobbying or pressure from alumni and fans—and sometimes even from trustees or regents. The board, as the final institutional authority, must ensure that the intercollegiate program is not allowed to take on a life of its own or to distort institutional priorities. It is tragic that on a few campuses board members with a particular interest in athletics have failed to support the president or chancellor in relationships with the athletic program. One of the great strengths of Notre Dame is that that has never been true here.

THE NCAA

Finally, let me offer a few thoughts about the NCAA—an organization some people view with distaste as a self-sustaining bureaucracy with a life of its own. Such fears stem from the fact that the NCAA has the power to redistribute significant amounts of money to cooperative institutions. The NCAA's critics also find the organization resistant to change and able to outlast reform-minded presidents and others who challenge its legitimacy and authority.

The problem with such criticisms is simply this: If the NCAA did not exist, it would have to be invented. Experience shows that institutions cooperate best when there is a collective agency to hold individual institutions to a common standard. The complexity of national tournaments in the various sports alone would warrant a fair bureaucracy. If you tack on negotiating radio and television contracts, and seeing to it that there are uniform standards in place across the campuses and conferences, you have a time-consuming and expensive task.

The efforts of the Knight Commission (a national panel put together by the Knight Foundation to recommend reforms in intercollegiate athletics) and the greater involvement of institutional presidents and chancellors in athletics have, I believe, set the NCAA going in the right direction. What is needed now is for the top leadership of the institutions to take the NCAA seriously. For myself, I take it for granted that we need a relatively independent agency to negotiate all this activity at the national level. With proper presidential involvement and periodic reviews by independent boards such as the Knight Commission, I believe the NCAA will continue to serve its purposes quite well. Two things that would probably give it greater credibility would be a mandated review of its rule book every so many years, and term limits for the central NCAA leadership. These two steps seem to me to be a proper path for future reform.

The NCAA has now mandated an accreditation review of individual campuses and their programs every ten years. Whatever the frequency, an accreditation review can, with the utilization of an outside reviewing group, promote honest and helpful internal conversation. Our recent experience at Notre Dame with such an accreditation was generally well received internally. We thought we had a good story to tell, and the evaluators agreed. But they also made a number of recommendations for improvement, which is as it should be in order that our program not have an exaggerated sense of its own quality.

Much of my firsthand experience of the NCAA is as a member of the NCAA Foundation, the organization's philanthropic arm. The foundation receives some money directly from the NCAA but also operates with funds solicited from corporations and individuals. These moneys are used to support several programs, including one that allows student-athletes to complete their degrees once their eligibility for athletic financial aid has elapsed. Other programs focus on leadership formation, alcohol and drug education, and the mentoring of youth.

Intercollegiate athletics opened up a new set of possibilities for me—it paid for my education, gave me the experience of both success and failure in a team context, provided the opportunity for travel, and helped me mature as a person. As both a participant and a fan, I enjoy sports. I like the thrill of competition, the spirited cheering for the team, the sights, sounds, and smells of collective endeavor toward a common goal with the outcome unknown until the end.

But at this moment of American higher education, intercollegiate athletics is also a complicated business, a challenge to academic and regulatory integrity, and sometimes the most visible way that a given institution receives attention from the media. At Notre Dame we have subdivided the administrative oversight of our athletic programs. As in all important matters, I retain final authority and responsibility. My work is eased considerably by Father E. William Beauchamp, C.S.C., our executive vice president, who deals more directly with the major administrative tasks including chairing the faculty board on athletics and serving as liaison to the Trustee Committee on Athletics. He supervises the athletic director, the coaches, and all the support personnel as well as the extensive physical plant. He also approves the budget and, with the athletic director, represents the university in the broader circles of intercollegiate athletics including the NCAA. I am pleased that Bill relieves me of so much of the concern for the day-to-day operation.

Other institutions will have their own evolved structures of administrative management and priority setting in athletics. No one style will work for all. The important thing is to recognize what a powerful force sports is in our culture and in our higher education institutions. It can be a force for good or ill. Together we must assure that this outcome is predetermined.

CHAPTER EIGHT

Religious Mission and Identity

Many of the most prominent private colleges and universities in this country, especially those east of the Mississippi
River, were founded under religious auspices: schools such
as Duke, Vanderbilt, Emory, Harvard, Yale, and Princeton.
Usually, the early presidents of these schools were minis-
ters, and among their duties were to lead worship, preach,
and give regular talks to the students on religious and moral
topics.

During the second great awakening in the early part of
the nineteenth century, many new colleges were founded
by the burgeoning Baptist and Methodist churches and
some of their break-off groups. Some had the mission of
providing educational opportunities for black people, for
women, for Native Americans, and for other deprived
groups. There was a deep conviction among Protestant
denominations that higher education is a good thing, and
that there's an obligation to make it available under religious auspices. Many of these institutions, some quite small,
became centers of their local communities.

The religiously inspired institutions that became prominent academically and grew in wealth and influence often shucked off their religious roots. Seldom did this happen after a public confrontation or an overt battle for dominance. Mostly, the process of secularization took place virtually by osmosis: At some point, the governing board or the administration or the president or the alumni or some combination thereof considered the religious heritage outdated. Soon mandatory chapel was eliminated, religious requirements for the presidency were abandoned, and the student code of conduct was liberalized.

Obviously, much of this was a result of forces in the country's broader cultural and intellectual life. In the post–scientific-revolution era, there developed a consensus that the day of the Protestant-affiliated school had passed. True, there are institutions that still prize their religious distinctiveness: Baylor University, Calvin College, Wheaton College, and Southern Methodist University are some. But on most of the prominent campuses, the explicitly religious dimension is now isolated in the divinity school or the university chapel or the campus ministry center. On certain public occasions a prayer might still be said, rendered in careful, nondenominational fashion, or the deity might be invoked in some traditional form. Sometimes religious figures are brought in to give a morally uplifting talk at commencement time. But no member of the board of trustees or central administration would confuse these remnants of the past with anything like a religious mission for the institution. And it would be highly suspect to bring any of this into the classroom.

CATHOLICS AND HIGHER EDUCATION

Although the first Catholic college in the United States, Georgetown University, dates to 1789, it was not until the middle to later years of the nineteenth century that America's Catholics had sufficient resources to start colleges in any numbers. Most were founded by religious communities of men and women, and those that survived did so out of great sacrifice and a deep conviction that their work was important; usually, survival involved overcoming fires, threats of insolvency, and sometimes negligent leadership. Catholic colleges for women are particularly noteworthy, since they provided opportunities for bright and talented women to serve as faculty and administrators, and they delivered high-quality education to young women long before it became a national priority. The surviving institutions make up today's American network of approximately 230 Catholic colleges and universities.

For much of their history, these institutions were centers of Catholic life and catechesis, and the role of the founding religious community was central and critical. In the vast majority of cases, the president of the institution was a member of the founding community, and so were many of its officers. The religious community owned the institution, and if lay boards existed, they served primarily as gatherings of potential benefactors.

Among the few Catholic colleges founded by local bishops, the governing structures of the local diocese took responsibility for the institution. The one variance from this pattern was the Catholic University of America. Founded in 1887, CUA was intended to be the "national" Catholic university, with a special emphasis on graduate education. It was expected that the Catholic laity in every diocese would provide support, and for many years the annual parish collections held for CUA were called "the living endowment."

FATHER SORIN'S VENTURE

The University of Notre Dame was founded in 1842 by Father Edward Sorin, C.S.C., and a group of Holy Cross brothers. Although it bore the title university from the beginning, it was primarily a grade school and high school in its early years, with limited offerings of college courses. It prevailed against such challenges as insufficient funds, an ill-prepared faculty, mosquito-borne diseases, and a tragic fire that burned down the Administration Building in 1879. After each setback, it made a new start. Today Notre Dame enjoys the largest endowment of any Catholic institution in the country, and a degree of academic prominence and financial stability that qualifies it as one of America's great universities.

From the vantage point of the end of the twentieth century, one can divide up the country's Catholic colleges and universities into various missions and spheres of influence. There are twenty-eight Jesuit institutions, many located in major metropolitan areas. There are nine Holy Cross–affiliated schools. A number of religious communities of women also have multiple institutions, among them the Ursulines, Dominicans, Franciscans, and Benedictines. Some Catholic institutions are full-fledged universities that compete with the country's prominent secular public and private universities. In addition to Notre Dame, this category would include Georgetown, Boston College, Catholic University, Fordham, Loyola of Chicago, DePaul, Saint Thomas, Loyola Marymount, Santa Clara, and Saint Louis. Others serve primarily a local population, and still others are regional institutions. There are four Catholic medical schools—Georgetown, Creighton, Saint Louis, and Loyola-Chicago—and a multiplicity of Catholic graduate schools, schools of education, and nursing schools. Some institutions serve heavily Hispanic or African-American population groups. What they all have in common is that they consider themselves Catholic and celebrate that religious heritage.

It is primarily since the 1960s, partly in the wake of Vatican II but also influenced by American cultural trends, that the Catholic nature of these institutions has come under question. Some Catholics fear that what happened to Protestant institutions will inevitably happen to theirs as well. Certainly there are no guarantees one way or another, but it may be useful to analyze the present scene and identify those variables that might impact the further evolution of Catholic colleges and universities.

A CATHOLIC PRESENCE

My own primary, secondary, and undergraduate education all took place in Catholic schools. The faculty at Saint Anthony's grade school in Washington, D.C., consisted entirely of Benedictine sisters. At Archbishop John Carroll High School there were a few lay teachers, but the vast majority were Augustinian priests and brothers. When I was an undergraduate at Notre Dame, although the majority of faculty were laymen, Holy Cross priests and brothers were active both in the classroom and the administration, and their most ubiquitous presence to students was in the dormitories where they served as rectors and assistant rectors.

A subculture abroad in the last decade or so has been quite busy churning out novels and plays that excoriate the treatment the writers received in Catholic schools. Some of this takes a humorous turn, but there's an underlying disenchantment in all of it. My own experience in three levels of Catholic education, by contrast, was overwhelmingly positive. I found the sisters, brothers, and priests, and the lay people as well, to be not only dedicated teachers but also human and humane mentors and counselors. Sister Eleanor, my teacher in the fourth, fifth, and sixth grades at Saint Anthony's, played a decisive role in my life, pushing me to succeed in classwork at a time when I had plenty of distractions. In high school, several priests went out of their way to both encourage and confront me at appropriate times. I look back at these mentors with real appreciation.

At Notre Dame I had excellent teachers and dedicated religious in the dorms who fostered a healthy student environment. There was no doubt during my undergraduate days that we were expected to meet fairly high standards of conduct, especially compared to students at some of the other institutions that I might have attended. During all my years as a student, questions of religious identity and mission would have seemed preposterous. We took it for granted that our parents had sent us to Catholic schools because they were different from public schools; they were places where academic standards were high and the whole person was cultivated. This meant an emphasis on extracurricular activities and regular religious exercises as well as on studies. Since I was an altar boy from the fifth grade on, I was in regular contact with priests of every age and stripe. I liked some of them more than others, but I shared with the vast majority of my peers an admiration and respect for these priest/mentors.

The disciplinary apparatus of these schools was an integral part of their Catholic nature. This meant that some activities were prohibited, and there was an implicit expectation that fair but unquestioned procedures of adjudication would follow any infractions. Up through my undergraduate experience, it was unheard of for parents not to back the faculty or administration.

Certain secondary characteristics distinguished the schools I attended. First, except for primary school, they were single-sex. This often meant, particularly at the high school and college level, an affiliation with some neighboring female institution for social events. Notre Dame's location right next door to Saint Mary's College was a big part of the social life of both institutions. A second feature of Catholic education at that time was the predominance of religious members on the faculty. Even at Notre Dame, the rough percentages of religious was higher then than it is in the complex institution we are today. And the principals and/or presidents of these institutions were members of the religious order.

A third feature was the emphasis on community. All

students were treated equally, no matter what their socioeconomic background. The wearing of standardized uniforms in grade school, and to a certain extent in high school, was one way of demonstrating this attitude. Even at Notre Dame it was hard to determine where anyone stood in the socioeconomic pecking order simply from observing them on campus. Manifest displays of wealth were considered gauche.

Finally, the explicitly religious dimension of these institutions was regularly expressed in common worship. Notre Dame encouraged daily Mass attendance and offered regular opportunities for the sacrament of Penance, retreats, and regular devotions to Our Lady of Lourdes at the Grotto. The dormitory chapels were constant reminders of the worship and prayer at the heart of the enterprise.

Perhaps the best way to summarize my experience of Saint Anthony's, Archbishop Carroll, and Notre Dame is to say that they were integrated institutions in which the Catholic view of reality was pervasive. Students received regular reminders that these places were deliberately different from state institutions and nonreligious private institutions. Catholic schools were not to everybody's taste, but for those who found the environment compatible, wonderful things happened in the development of the life of the mind, integrated into the life of faith.

GOVERNANCE CHANGES

In 1967 the Congregation of Holy Cross, with the approval of the Vatican, created a new institutional entity at Notre Dame called the Board of Trustees and made it the effective owner of the school. It simultaneously formed a group called the Fellows, made up of six Holy Cross priests of the Indiana Province and six lay people. This latter group was entrusted with preserving the university's Catholic character and mission, with approving the appointment of all trustees, and with ratifying, by a two-thirds vote, any changes in the bylaws. The fellows were also charged with paying special attention to the continuing role of the Congregation of Holy Cross in the university's administrative ranks, dorm work, campus ministry, and departments of philosophy and theology.

Other Catholic universities were going through similar transformations at about the same time, for many of the same reasons. The change was in conformity with the spirit of the Second Vatican Council and the greater emphasis it placed on the role of Catholic lay people in all aspects of church life. Also, many religious communities were experiencing declining numbers, a problem to which no Catholic institution is immune. Since some of the structural change was driven by theological rationales distinct from personnel questions, it is important to say here that the changes at Notre Dame and many other places have generally been quite successful. It is difficult to find much evidence that governing boards of Catholic colleges, although made up of fewer religious than they once had, are failing in their responsibility to preserve Catholic identity and mission. In fact, one might make the case that some religious communities have failed their institutions by refusing to alter the structures of government toward greater lay collaboration.

It is my conviction that the change in 1967 at Notre

Dame was the proper and right thing to do. This university is a better place under the new governing structure. We have found a good mix between the preservative function of the fellows and the more encompassing responsibilities of the trustees. We have also enjoyed a succession of outstanding board chairs. So far as I am aware, this has been true as well at most other major Catholic universities.

This success, of course, is no guarantee that it will continue. The backgrounds of new board members will change to reflect the varying circumstances in American culture and church life. A growing percentage of members is likely to have gone through divorce and sometimes remarriage, which can affect their attitudes toward the institutional church. A higher percentage is liable to be in mixed-religious marriages. Their experience of church, both in terms of parish life and diocesan spirit, can vary considerably.

Keeping the Faith

Since it is crucial that board members fully embrace their school's Catholic identity and mission, they must be well chosen and properly instructed. This usually means a formal procedure to acquaint new members not only with procedural matters but also with a theological rationale for Catholic identity. Very few of the boards of modern Catholic institutions are entirely Catholic, yet it would seem desirable for them to be heavily so, not only in name but also in the life commitments of the members. Let me add quickly, however, that in my experience non-Catholic members of boards are often the strongest advocates and defenders of religious specificity.

It is absolutely essential that the governing boards of Catholic institutions play strong roles in ensuring that the institution not lose its way. The board's leadership should consider this focus a fundamental responsibility, and the full board should remind itself constantly that the distinctiveness of Catholic institutions is their greatest strength. It goes without saying that board meetings should begin and end with prayer and that there should be an opportunity for the celebration of the Eucharist. The board, in short, should be a microcosm of the institutional spirit. While the local bishop normally has no formal role in the governing boards of Catholic colleges and universities, it is important that the board relate with him comfortably and in friendly fashion. This is one way of manifesting the Catholic character of the institution, as well as avoiding unnecessary controversy. At Notre Dame, we have had excellent relationships with our local ordinaries.

The central administration is another key element in safeguarding the religious identity and mission of an institution. As far as I know, all the Catholic institutions in the United States now have a practicing Catholic as president or chancellor. When presidencies were restricted to members of the founding religious congregation or to a priest of the founding diocese, the issue of religious diversity simply did not arise. Today, the central question is not simply whether the chief executive officer of a religiously affiliated institution is a card-carrying member of the particular community of faith—what's imperative is that he or she has incorporated the value system that is central to the nature of the institution. And it is one of the responsibilities of the governing board, in choosing a new president, to assure that religious character and identity are at the forefront of the presidential responsibilities.

On the basis of my experience I would argue that it is self-evident that the leader of a Catholic institution must be a Catholic. Perhaps extraordinary circumstances might warrant another choice, but a strong case would have to be made. I also believe the majority of central administrators should be Catholics as well. It is important that they have a firsthand and lived experience of the Catholic faith community.

Having said that, let me acknowledge that at Notre Dame, the present provost and second officer of the university, Nathan Hatch, is not a Catholic. Although his choice elicited some measure of wonderment, I know of no one in our administration who is more thoroughly committed to Notre Dame's Catholic character. He believes deeply in the importance of religiously affiliated institutions in the spectrum of higher education, and he has had long experience at Notre Dame as a faculty member and administrator. I was chair of the search committee that chose him, and I was—and am—convinced he was the best candidate for the position, including the crucial dimension of the Catholic presence in the intellectual world of the university. There must always be some flexibility in selecting central administrators. At present, all the deans of Notre Dame's colleges are Catholic, but a few major administrators are not. Each institution has to chart its own way when it comes to the right mix.

A related question has to do with members of religious communities serving in central leadership roles. By their

presence they symbolize the religious nature of the institution. As president of Notre Dame, I have manifold opportunities to lead the university community in prayer
and to explicitly invoke religious values in our common
life and activities. The same would be true to some extent if I were a religious brother or sister. None of this is
said to underappreciate the wonderful leadership being
provided in Catholic institutions by Catholic lay administrators. It is simply to say that there are advantages to
having some portion of the administration perceived by
all as carriers of the religious identity of the institution.

One of the dangers of putting too much emphasis on
the religious commitments of administrators is that some
may undergo dramatic changes in their life situation while
exercising their role. This can happen when members of
religious communities are released from their vows, or
priests are laicized, or lay Catholics go through the trauma
of divorce and possibly remarriage. I mention these matters simply to acknowledge that in the human condition,
changes in people's lives sometimes influence their ability to provide successful leadership in a religiously affiliated institution.

Another danger is that members of religious communities or dioceses can remain too long in leadership positions because of difficulty in finding replacements from
the same communities. While there is both symbolic and
real importance to preserving the linkage between a Jesuit institution and in the society of Jesus, or between a
Holy Cross–affiliated college and the Congregation of Holy
Cross, no one would go so far as to argue for keeping a
member of a religious community in leadership if it works

to the detriment of the institution. All things being equal, I believe in preserving the linkage with an institution's founding religious community by having members of these communities in central leadership roles, including the presidency. The community is the greatest source of continuity between the past, the present, and the future. But if time and good evidence dictate that this is no longer possible, then an appropriate change ought to be made in the bylaws or traditions of the institution.

THE FACULTY

At one level, there is no more self-evident proposition than the desirability of having the majority of the faculty be active participants in the institution's religious tradition. This is no different than proposing that the majority of faculty at a women's college be women or the majority of faculty at a historically black college or university be African-Americans. There is much in any culture that's transmitted by osmosis through shared experience.

It must also be acknowledged that nothing is more alien to the hiring practices of American higher education than taking religion into account. Many professional societies have tried to legislate against ever asking about religious preferences—as if religion were a peripheral thing that has nothing to do with scholarship or commitment to teaching or striving for intellectual excellence. A certain percentage of academics are, if not overtly hostile to religion, at least suspicious of its aims and purposes. They would find it surprising that a Nobel Prize winner in physics or chemistry might be an active member of a faith community, and they would be skeptical that great art or music or creative expression could be generated by anyone who was not rebelling against a religious background. Some have spoken about "the cultured despisers of religion." When Auguste Comte, the French positivist philosopher, predicted that science would eventually replace religion, he captured that perspective.

My view is far different. I am convinced that whether or not one is a religious person makes a huge difference in one's vision of life and one's capacity to draw connections among all the fields of learning. To claim that the search for the truth is not only reconcilable with the life of faith but an essential component of it is to probe the central purpose of our existence in this world. To come out of a long-standing faith community like the Catholic Christian Church is to be the inheritor of a legacy. It means none of us has to start from scratch—we can put ourselves in touch with the learning of the ages, thus motivating us to carry on comparable tasks in the present.

To be a believer is to be on a perpetual quest for greater understanding—not in radical isolation but in connectedness with other believers, both contemporary and historical. Augustine and Thomas Aquinas were concerned about fundamental things. Martin Luther and John Calvin wanted to purify the practicing faith community of their day. Theresa of Avilla and John of the Cross sought to make the richness of Christianity's spiritual heritage more fully available. In our own day too, people of strong faith can be found in all fields of professional and scholarly endeavor. Some, it's true, maintain a degree of shyness or personal silence about the connection between their faith

and their profession. But in the face of the heavily prejudicial overlay of the contemporary academy, I feel it's important to reassert the significance of religion, not only
as a way of charging one's vocational sense but as the very
foundation for all of one's professional activity.

Counting Catholics

On May 7, 1993, I submitted a report to the trustees of
Notre Dame entitled *Colloquy for the Year 2000*. It was the
product of more than two years of discussion by a representative cross section of faculty, staff, students, and administrators. The document contained analyses of all
major areas of university life and offered forty-three concrete recommendations. The exercise was intended to satisfy one of the requirements for our ten-year, institution-
wide accreditation review and also to enable us to put in
place the elements, including dollar figures, of our next
major fundraising effort. But the *Colloquy* was something
more—an attempt to articulate as clearly as possible the
challenges and opportunities that Notre Dame faces at
this moment of its history.

Because we are religiously affiliated, I thought it desirable to begin the document with a section on the school's
Catholic character, and I began with a bold assertion:
". . . [T]he Catholic mission and character of Notre
Dame are its greatest strengths and the main reason that
the future is bright and full of promise." Because of that,
I asserted, "the University must pay special attention to
the central elements of this religious heritage, so that the
inevitable demand for change might be seen as an oppor-

tunity for greater enrichment and not as a betrayal of a sacred trust."

The twin dangers facing Catholic higher education today, I'm convinced, are the societal trend toward secularization on the one hand, and too narrow a conceptualization of what constitutes a Catholic institution on the other. Notre Dame can never be relegated to the status of a seminary or a catechetical institute or a bureaucratic function of the church; it must be a full-fledged university in all important senses of the term. Yet it must also be a full-fledged *Catholic* university.

There were twin dangers in raising this theme explicitly in the *Colloquy* report. One was that some members of the Notre Dame community might feel excluded or underappreciated. That's why I went on to make it clear that all are welcomed and honored at Notre Dame. We are an ecumenical community in the best sense of the term; in performance evaluation and the assignment of merit, everyone is treated according to commonly recognized standards of fairness and equity. The second danger comes in applying the principle, and that's where two of the *Colloquy's* forty-three recommendations ran into considerable campus reaction.

One stated: "In recruiting new faculty, each department must make energetic efforts to hire faculty of the highest caliber to seek to participate in the intellectual life of a dynamic Catholic university. All who participate in hiring faculty must be cognizant of and responsive to the need for dedicated and committed Catholics to predominate in number among the faculty." The second read: "In the interest of sustaining and developing the Catholic character of the University, it is anticipated that the Congregation of Holy Cross will continue to emphasize academic careers, and it is recommended that the University give special consideration in personnel decisions, consistent with prevailing standards of excellence, to the Congregation's unique role at Notre Dame."

Although both recommendations reiterated themes that had appeared often in earlier planning documents, the first of the two in particular drew criticism, especially from our faculty senate. There is no denying that the question of standards used in hiring faculty is a complicated and difficult one. The passive strain of thought in some Catholic institutions is that there's no need to ask candidates explicitly about their religious affiliation or philosophy of life because one can take for granted that Catholics will be attracted to apply at Catholic institutions. This view assumes that the marketplace will see to it that some degree of success in the hiring of Catholic faculty will occur without explicit attention being paid to the matter.

I am aware of no evidence to support this position. In recent years, many more graduates of doctoral programs have been entering the marketplace than there are positions available. Under those circumstances, it seems clear to me that a candidate is far more likely to focus on the concreteness of a job offer than on an adjectival description like "Catholic institution." Schools with higher salary scales, more positions, better institutional financial health, and a higher academic reputation will be the ones attracting the top candidates. In short, if the question about religious affiliation were never raised in the hiring process, Notre Dame's faculty would eventually come to look very much like the faculty at our secular peer institutions.

It's true that an inquiry about religious affiliation may not tell very much about the candidate. At Notre Dame we simply ask that the religion box be filled out according to the candidate's own sense of things, which means that the answer could be Catholic, Roman Catholic, Protestant, Lutheran, Hindu, Buddhist, Jewish, or none. There are no orthodoxy tests, so those filling out the Catholic box may or may not be dedicated and committed members of the faith. Nevertheless, having candidates provide a self-description is at least a starting point that provides a rough idea of how a cross section of faculty members in a given department or college or university-wide thinks of itself on religious grounds. In the absence of this minimal information, the composition of the faculty could change drastically over time without anyone being aware of it.

On the basis of evidence gathered in the hiring process, there has already been a decline in the percentage of our faculty who describe themselves as Catholic. For many years, slightly more than 60 percent overall were self-described Catholics. That percentage has been going down. Hence the *Colloquy's* call for "dedicated and committed Catholics to predominate in number among the faculty."

THE HEART OF THE MATTER

The precise definition of "predominate" was at the heart of objections to that recommendation. At face value it would mean at least one more than 50 percent, but my intention was less numerical than philosophical; it expressed my desire that the overall faculty continue to include a sufficient percentage of Catholics so that its Catholic identity and mission might be fully manifest. Alternative phrase-ology during the discussion that shaped the report con-sidered and rejected terms such as "a sufficient number" or "a critical mass." The problem with those phrases is that they're so ambiguous it would be difficult to apply any test over time to measure success or failure. In the eyes of some, a mere 10 percent of the faculty could be a critical mass.

A related problem is an uneven distribution of Catholic faculty across the disciplines. There seem to be more in the humanities, law, and business than in the natural or social sciences, and more in architecture and engineering than in the performing arts. The reasons are difficult to sort out. Nor is it clear whether this situation is tempo-rary or permanent. What it means in today's market is that the various academic units must make every effort to maximize the pool of Catholics in the hiring process, and that they evaluate their success over time.

Since the *Colloquy* report was disseminated, Provost Nathan Hatch has developed a new strategy in the dis-tribution of potential faculty positions. This policy re-stricts one-third of all new positions to strategic targets of opportunity—Catholics, women, members of histori-cal minority groups, and Holy Cross religious—the vari-ous academic units can then compete for positions when they have qualified candidates that fulfill one or more of these criteria. We are already seeing positive results from this approach, and I'm hopeful that we can mobilize the university community to make further progress toward our goal.

Once the hiring judgments are made, let me repeat, we are committed to treating all faculty members equally in every stage of review. In fact, we no longer cite religious affiliation in the packet that goes up for promotion; not only would that be dishonorable on the general grounds of equity and fairness, but it also acknowledges the fact that people can change their religious preference after joining the faculty. Some self-described Catholics have come to Notre Dame with a cynical view of the church, only to find that their experience of the university as a faith community leads them to become heavily involved in the worship life of the campus. Others who have arrived here as committed Catholics have gone through changes such as divorce and remarriage that raise serious questions about their status within the life of the church. Still others have become disenchanted by some teachings of the hierarchical church or some experience they've had in the community of faith. Whether such life changes are positive or negative with regard to religious identity, it is all but inevitable that a self-description provided at the time of hiring will not remain static.

Where's the Difference?

Even those who accept the importance of concern for religious identity in the hiring process may still find it hard to understand what difference religious affiliation can or should make in the exercise of professorial responsibilities. Is there such a thing as Catholic mathematics? Catholic chemistry? For me the answer is both no and yes. While some disciplines such as art, sociology, philosophy, architecture, and law have a historical connection to religion that flows out of their history and methodology, others are so mathematically based or oblivious to subjective concerns that it appears there can be no direct connection between religion and the way the course content is approached.

This is a complicated question. A number of wise analysts have pointed out that the claim for value-neutrality underlying contemporary science is not as self-evident as it's been taken to be, because the questions posed by the observer of any phenomenon influence the answers. When a believer asserts that the search for the truth is a legitimate path to God, that's a philosophical/theological claim of the highest order which suggests the biologist, the mechanical engineer, the psychologist, and the historian are all engaged in a vocational pursuit of rich significance.

As for the question of whether there is a Catholic version of some disciplines, the bald answer is "no," but the fuller answer is that in the subjective world of the faculty member, there are always possibilities of interconnection and application that bring into play the explicit value framework of the believing person. The astronomer who gazes into the heavens as a believer can discern the handiwork of God, and this can be a part of the personal grounding of that astronomer's life and work. The sociologist who instructs students about the significance of tribal identities and socioeconomic structures can call attention to a whole range of justice issues that flow from such analyses. The biologist who explains the evolving capacity for human intervention in the propagation of the species can raise questions about the desirability and ethics of such activity. We are neither thinking machines nor objective automatons; what we are is complex individuals who bring our fundamental values and life experiences into everything we do. The minimal claim I would assert is that concern about religious identity is consistent with this view of faculty members as full human agents.

Not only is it important to have dedicated and committed Catholics on the faculty, but it is also important to facilitate a broader conversation across disciplines. Ideally, Catholic intellectual life on a campus like Notre Dame would be full of targeted research projects, vigorous exchange, and ongoing mutual support. It would never be restricted in any way simply to Catholic faculty, but it would welcome the engagement of other Christian faculty, or any faculty who share similar concerns. At various times, apart from any administrative initiatives, we have had faculty-sponsored efforts to bring interested persons together to talk freely about matters that engage their minds and hearts as committed believers. Participants tell me these conversations have been very helpful, not only in the quality of the discussions but also in the friendships they've spawned. While some observers have viewed these discussions as divisive, or as a way of promoting a narrow frame of reference for the intellectual debate, my opinion is that they have been quite fruitful.

It is good for scholars, who often live fairly isolated lives, to come together at least occasionally for high-order conversation about substantive and meaty questions that are difficult to resolve and admit a wide variety of perspectives toward a tentative conclusion. Whether it is an intergenerational responsibility in the broad field of ecology or the essential elements of good government or the proper use of technology or the theoretical underpinning of integrity in the professions, there are issues that stand in need of a clarification of terminology and an openness to a variety of theoretical perspectives. Faculty members from an explicitly religious tradition may have a special concern for an updating that is theologically sophisticated and grounded in the best and most persuasive theoretical framework.

A Catholic university can be the most exciting of intellectual contexts for faculty and students alike. There are literally no questions that lie outside the realm of discussion. Since, in secular settings, religious questions are often pooh-poohed or rendered irrelevant, it can legitimately be claimed that a Catholic university is more open than its secular counterparts, and not less.

CENTERS AND INSTITUTES

One way a Catholic university can promote the development of Catholic intellectual life is by creating centers and institutes. My predecessor, Father Hesburgh, established a number of such entities connected directly to Notre Dame's Catholic identity and mission. The Ecumenical Institute in Tantur, Israel, promotes discussion among the Christian churches; by virtue of its location, it facilitates interreligious dialogue as well. The Kroc Peace Institute on our campus offers not only degrees in peace studies but also regular symposia and conferences that concentrate on particular regions of the world and forms of conflict resolution. Our Kellogg Institute focuses on Latin America, including such matters as church-state relations, economic justice, and participatory democracy. The Center for Civil and Human Rights in our law school has a concern for systems of accountability in various nations and cultures that are troubled by internal conflict and corrupt leadership.

In addition, UNDERC (the University of Notre Dame's Ecological Research Center) in Land O' Lakes, Wisconsin, offers research opportunities to students and faculty in the broad area of aquatic biology and ecology. The Snite Museum of Art, in its permanent collection and in the special shows that it hosts, can also highlight themes related to the institution's Catholic identity. The campus-based Cushwa Center for the Study of American Catholicism, the Center for Philosophy of Religion, the Hesburgh Program in Public Service, and the Program in Science Technology and Values are all related in some way to the fundamental issue of institutional identity and mission. Finally, Notre Dame Press provides a vehicle for ongoing scholarly discussion of a number of important areas of study.

Another way in which a place like Notre Dame can be a center for Catholic intellectual life is through service to the church at large. Our Institute for Church Life is an umbrella organization that oversees the Center for Social Concerns, whose mission is to promote a high level of volunteerism by our student body; the Center for Pastoral Liturgy, which offers programming for local church communities; and Retreats International, an organization for those involved in retreat work around the globe. In addition, Notre Dame frequently plays host to the Catholic Bishops Conference and provides specialized study opportunities for newly consecrated bishops. The Catholic university, in the best sense of the term, is one that not only serves its internal constituency and the broader academy, but also supports the Catholic Church and other interested faith communities.

Notre Dame's Alumni Association is an additional vehicle for service through its off-campus programming. For example, the Hesburgh Lecture Series dispatches distinguished Notre Dame faculty to all parts of the country for lectures and discussions. The Alumni Association also sponsors teleconference programs that can involve participants in distant settings. And Golden Dome Productions assists the university's outreach efforts by producing half-hour programs on a variety of contemporary issues—a service that responds to the need for high-quality television programming.

POLICIES

One of the most controversial areas of university life that puts our religious identity and mission to the test is university policies. An example is our investment policy, which not only precludes us from investing in companies engaged in harmful activities but explicitly forbids investment in companies that produce products or services that contradict church teaching. Another has to do with companies that manufacture athletic equipment or apparel carrying the Notre Dame logo. We want to be sure these firms do not engage in unfair labor practices or tolerate dangerous working conditions. A third policy area has to do with our desire to be an affirmative action employer and to foster opportunities for staff promotion and advancement.

Perhaps the touchiest policy area has to do with giving recognition to student organizations. At Notre Dame, formal recognition includes not only the provision of office space and, usually, some budgetary support, but also the ability to bring in speakers and reserve university space for events. In a sense, then, the formal recognition of a group is tantamount to university support and a semblance of endorsement of the group's activities.

For this reason, we have refused to give recognition to student groups that, by their own definition or in their potential activity, might advocate positions that run counter to church teaching. This is something entirely apart from the open acceptance of a variety of points of view in the classroom, in faculty-sponsored lectures or symposia, or in the exercise of faculty academic prerogatives. It involves not academic freedom but university endorsement of positions that diverge from those which flow from our religious identity. For instance, some other Catholic schools have had problems with student groups espousing a pro-abortion position. That has not been true at Notre Dame; what we've been faced with lately is efforts to organize a student group around matters concerning sexual identity.

After considerable discussion in the media and efforts by campus bodies to have the university recognize a gay and lesbian group, we have chosen another path by putting in place informal groups, under the sponsorship of the Student Affairs office and Campus Ministry, to bring together gay and lesbian students for purposes of mutual support and the exploration of issues related to sexual identity. The reason for this restriction has been a concern about the ability of the university to either influence or control the activities of such a group once it's formally recognized. The experience of other campuses suggests that this is more than a theoretical concern.

In a similar vein, there have been efforts to prod the university to include sexual orientation in its formal nondiscrimination clause. We have chosen not to do so because institutional nondiscrimination clauses are highly stylized and legally binding statements. Neither federal nor state law mandates including sexual orientation in these clauses, and we would prefer not to have the civil courts interpret the significance of such a change through the lens of the broader society in which we live. This, we feel, could jeopardize our ability to make decisions we believe necessary to support church teaching.

In place of adding sexual orientation to our nondiscrimination language, we have adopted a statement called "The Spirit of Inclusion at Notre Dame." This statement, which is argued with a strong theological rationale appropriate to a Catholic institution, states among other things: "The University of Notre Dame strives for a spirit of inclusion among the members of this community for distinct reasons in our Christian tradition. We prize the uniqueness of all persons as God's creatures. We welcome all people, regardless of color, religion, ethnicity, sexual orientation, social or economic class, and nationality, for example, precisely because of Christ's calling to treat others as we desire to be treated. We value gay and lesbian members of this community as we value all members of this community. We condemn harassment of any kind, and University policies proscribe it. We consciously create an environment of mutual respect and hospitality and warmth in which none are strangers and all may flourish."

We believe this states in the strongest possible terms the standards by which we want to hold ourselves accountable. It also allows us to distinguish, as the society around us often does not, between homosexual persons and homosexual conduct. While there are wide differences of opinion about this matter even within Christian communities, we believe Catholic teaching is quite clear: All people, regardless of their sexual orientation, are called to live chaste lives in accordance with their vocations as single people, married people, priests, or religious. Specifically, the church asks us all to reserve sexual union until the convenanted and consecrated union of a man and woman occurs in marriage.

I'm sure we'll continue to face other difficult issues when formulating and articulating policy. In a community with a diverse student body, faculty, and staff, not everyone agrees with the priority we place on matters like religious affiliation, but I am convinced that it is necessary for us to pay close attention to the way we project ideals for ourselves as a university community, and the ways in which we draw connections between our religious heritage and our ongoing life and practices.

Ex Corde Ecclesiae

For seven years and more, I've been among the university leaders involved in an ongoing, worldwide discussion about the responsibilities of an institution of Catholic higher education. I served on two different commissions that met in the Vatican to prepare for a papal statement on the topic. Serving with me were representatives from Catholic institutions all over the world, as well as bishops

and other church leaders. The final document issued by
Pope John Paul II was called *Ex Corde Ecclesiae* or, in English, "From the Heart of the Church." Overall, it is an
inspiring letter.

In it there is an expectation that national groupings of
bishops will initiate a process to prepare explicit application of the document to their particular culture. In response, the American Catholic bishops established a committee of bishops and presidential advisers to fashion an
application in the context of American Catholic higher
education, and I have had the privilege of serving in this
group as well. The early efforts of this committee were
somewhat frustrating because of a wide perception gap
between the bishops and the presidents about what was
needed. But once open discussions were held, the quality
of the give-and-take improved significantly. Bishop John
Leibrecht proved an outstanding committee chair who kept
this effort going in a spirit of unity. Father Terry Toland,
S.J., former president of Saint Joseph University in Philadel-
phia, was an excellent *peritus* for the committee.

After long study and deliberation, the committee came
forward with a document that won near-unanimous support from the bishops at one of their annual meetings.
Unfortunately, when the document was sent to Rome,
there was a request for significant alterations, and the final
shape of the American implementation materials is not
yet known at this writing.

The most critical issue in this discussion has been the
notion that Catholic theologians must seek a mandate
granting formal church approval of their role within colleges or universities. The notion of a mandate, a canoni-

cal term, is highly objectionable to most Catholic faculty members and institutional leaders, because it seems a throwback to a harsher day in church life and a level of hierarchical involvement in institutions that is neither historically accurate in the American context nor, in my judgment, necessary.

The main problem is that it suggests a level of suspicion about the proper role of the theologian in the Catholic university. This in no way springs from any level of difficulty in Catholic higher education in the United States, where the vast majority of theologians function well and effectively, not only teaching in the classrooms and publishing in scholarly journals, but also leading workshops and conferences and in many cases assisting local bishops and church agencies in their dealings with matters of doctrine, liturgy, ethics, and social service.

Aside from the question of whether a mandate is desirable, there is a practical question: How could it ever be properly exercised? Most bishops are not trained theologians, and they lack the professional qualifications to review faculty theologians. In most cases they would have to delegate this task to someone else, which raises the further question of whom they might call upon. In addition, there are many subfields within Catholic theology, all of which involve a degree of specialized expertise. Since even the well-trained bishop/theologian would not normally have competence across all theological subdisciplines, it is likely that inordinate attention would be given to some fields as opposed to others, which would be manifestly unfair.

There are plenty of opportunities already in place for

local bishops to critique the work of theologians when they believe it necessary. This can also be done by the National Conference of Bishops and by the various agencies of the Vatican. If questions need to be raised about the orthodoxy or reliability of a Catholic theologian, there is no limit to the publicly available means to communicate that information. Meanwhile, it is important to preserve within the university the high standards of academic freedom and scholarly inquiry that are at the heart of the enterprise. This must apply to theologians as well as to faculty in other disciplines. While bishops, along with the Holy Father, properly carry responsibility for insuring the orthodoxy of church teaching, their role is different from that of theologians. The university must be preserved as a place where unpopular opinions can be expressed, where inquiry can take surprising directions, and where the opportunity for more appropriate articulation of the life of faith can be pursued with vigor and integrity.

A mandate for Catholic theologians is simply a bad idea. It goes against the grain of the established practices of Catholic higher education in this country, and it contradicts the appropriate level of semi-autonomy that institutions must enjoy in order to serve the church properly. With respectful and regular conversation between university administrators and church authorities, problems can be kept to a minimum and the separate but related roles preserved.

The local bishop should always be a welcome visitor whose advice and concerns are taken seriously. But his role is different from that of the university president, officers, or governing board. When all of the above are attending diligently to the nature of a Catholic institution, the chances are greatest that the Catholic identity and mission will be preserved in all their glory, and the college or university will fully serve the church in its unique fashion.

CONCLUDING REFLECTION

Among all the strengths of American culture, none has more long-range significance for the well-being of the national and world society than the network of approximately 3,500 institutions of higher education. These schools come in all shapes and sizes, with varying formal identities and governance structures. In my judgment it is the richness and diversity of these schools (in their complexity, in their accessibility, and in their quality) that constitutes the uniqueness of this American effort. We have a federal Department of Education but no Minister of Education. We have, on the public side, support from local, state, and federal sources but no uniformity of expectation. We have accrediting agencies but no super-agency to thwart the available creative energy and spirit.

Well established within this broader system of institutional relationships are the 230 Catholic colleges and universities. They are one of the great achievements of the Catholic community at any time or place in its history. They are collectively a potent source for good for both society and the church.

In a narrower frame of reference, I know best from my firsthand experience the University of Notre Dame. It is,

I believe, a university with a rare opportunity to manifest the best that the American traditions and practices of higher education represent while maintaining and enhancing its distinctive religious roots and mission. The temptations are many and the path is not assured. But in God's grace I pray that we are worthy of the challenge.